CW00701482

# Crossing Barriers and Bridging Cultures

## Other Books of Interest

About Translation
  *Peter Newmark*
Annotated Texts for Translation: English – German
  *Christina Schäffner with Uwe Wiesemann*
'Behind Inverted Commas': Translation and Anglo-German Cultural Relations in the Nineteenth Century
  *Susanne Stark*
Constructing Cultures: Essays on Literary Translation
  *Susan Bassnett and André Lefevere*
Contemporary Translation Theories (2nd Edition)
  *Edwin Gentzler*
Culture Bumps: An Empirical Approach to the Translation of Allusions
  *Ritva Leppihalme*
Linguistic Auditing
  *Nigel Reeves and Colin Wright*
Literary Translation: A Practical Guide
  *Clifford E. Landers*
More Paragraphs on Translation
  *Peter Newmark*
Paragraphs on Translation
  *Peter Newmark*
Practical Guide for Translators
  *Geoffrey Samuelsson-Brown*
The Coming Industry of Teletranslation
  *Minako O'Hagan*
The Interpreter's Resource
  *Mary Phelan*
The Pragmatics of Translation
  *Leo Hickey (ed.)*
The Rewriting of Njäls Saga: Translation, Ideology, and Icelandic Sagas
  *Jón Karl Helgason*
Translation, Power, Subversion
  *Román Álvarez and M. Carmen-África Vidal (eds)*
Translation and Nation: A Cultural Politics of Englishness
  *Roger Ellis and Liz Oakley-Brown (eds)*
Translation-mediated Communication in a Digital World
  *Minako O'Hagan and David Ashworth*
Time Sharing on Stage: Drama Translation in Theatre and Society
  *Sirkku Aaltonen*
Word, Text, Translation: *Liber Amicorum* for Peter Newmark
  *Gunilla Anderman and Margaret Rogers (eds)*

**Please contact us for the latest book information:**
Multilingual Matters, Frankfurt Lodge, Clevedon Hall,
Victoria Road, Clevedon, BS21 7HH, England
http://www.multilingual-matters.com

drafting?languages - English + french.

# Crossing Barriers and Bridging Cultures

## The Challenges of Multilingual Translation for the European Union

Edited by
**Arturo Tosi**

**MULTILINGUAL MATTERS LTD**
Clevedon • Buffalo • Toronto • Sydney

**Library of Congress Cataloging in Publication Data**
Crossing Barriers and Bridging Cultures: The Challenges of Multilingual Translation
for the European Union/Edited by Arturo Tosi
Includes bibliographical references and index.
1. Translating and interpreting–Europe. 2. Multilingualism–Political aspects–Europe.
3. Languages in contact–Europe. 4. European Union. I. Tosi, Arturo.
P306.8.E85 C76 2001
418′.02′094–dc21   2002021933

**British Library Cataloguing in Publication Data**
A catalogue entry for this book is available from the British Library.

ISBN 1-85359-604-3 (hbk)
ISBN 1-85359-603-5 (pbk)

**Multilingual Matters Ltd**
*UK*: Frankfurt Lodge, Clevedon Hall, Victoria Road, Clevedon BS21 7HH.
*USA*: UTP, 2250 Military Road, Tonawanda, NY 14150, USA.
*Canada*: UTP, 5201 Dufferin Street, North York, Ontario M3H 5T8, Canada.
*Australia*: Footprint Books, PO Box 418, Church Point, NSW 2103, Australia.

Published on behalf of the EU Translation Service by Multilingual Matters Ltd.

Typeset by Archetype-IT Ltd (http://www.archetype-it.com).
Printed and bound in Great Britain by the Cromwell Press Ltd.

# Contents

# The Contributors

**Sylvia Ball** holds a BA Hons degree in French and Italian and a PhD from the University of Sheffield. She has worked in the Translation Service of the European Parliament as a terminologist since 1982, currently as leader of the terminology team in the SILD (IT, Language and Documentation Support) Division.

**Nicole Buchin** is currently a translator at the European Parliament. She has taken part in the two seminars, one on multilingualism and one on multi-culturalism, organised by the institution.

**Christopher Cook** joined the BBC in 1969. He worked in the Documentary Department making films for BBC-2 Television and then produced and directed for Channel 4 Television, including the series on British politics in the 1970s, '*The Writing on the Wall*'. For over 20 years now he has written and presented programmes for BBC Radios 2, 3, 4 and 5 and the BBC World Service. He currently teaches Cultural Studies on the London Programme of Syracuse University.

**Renato Correia** is a translator at the European Parliament. Until 1993 he was lecturer at Coimbra University, where he helped organise in 1987 one of the first postgraduate courses for translators in Portugal. He has several publications on literature, literary translation, translation theory, translation history and the language arrangements of the European institutions.

**Freddie De Corte** was Freelance Conference Interpreter and Chargé de Cours at the School for Translators and Interpreters, Lessiushogeschool, Antwerp until 1987. Since 1988 he has been Senior Translator (French, Italian, German, Portuguese into Dutch) in the Dutch Translation Division, European Parliament, Luxembourg.

**Christopher Rollason** graduated with First Class Honours in English Literature from Trinity College, Cambridge in 1975, and obtained his PhD from York University in 1988. He spent eight years as a member of the Department of Anglo-American Studies of the Faculty of Letters of Coimbra University (Portugal). He became a European Parliament official in 1987, and currently holds the rank of Senior Translator in the English Translation Division.

**Edward Seymour** has been a translator at the European Parliament for 25 years. His particular interests include the interplay between writing and translation, legal language and clarity, and 'native' and Euro-English. His translation of Goethe's verse drama *Iphigenie auf Tauris* was published by Playscripts.com in June 2002.

**Helen Swallow** is a translator in the English Translation Division of the European Parliament. She has many years' experience of translation, lexicography and English language teaching, including a period as Assistant Lecturer at the Université Catholique de Louvain at Louvain-la-Neuve, where she co-authored *Un dictionnaire des faux amis français-anglais* with Jacques Van Roey and Sylviane Granger (pub. Duculot, Paris-Gembloux).

**Luca Tomasi** began his career as a freelance translator in 1982. He joined the Translation Service of the European Commission in Brussels in 1990. After two years in President Prodi's Cabinet, in March 2002 he moved to the Language Policy Unit of the Commission's Directorate-General for Education and Culture.

**Arturo Tosi** is Professor of Italian at Royal Holloway, University of London and Visiting Professor of Sociolinguistics in Italy at the Università di Studi di Siena. He has published widely in the fields of bilingualism and bilingual education, contact-linguistics, translation, multilingualism and language policy in Europe.

**John L.M. Trim** was first Director of the Department of Linguistics of Cambridge University, then Director of CILT and Director of the Modern Languages Projects of the Council of Europe 1971–1997. Now retired, he maintains an active professional interest in many branches of applied linguistics, particularly language policy.

**Anne Tucker** works as a computational linguist at the European Parliament with responsibility for the definition, deployment and support of computer tools used in the Translation Directorate. She was previously employed as a translator at the European Parliament. She holds degrees in Modern Languages, Translation Studies, Mathematics and Computing Science.

**Barry Wilson** studied Modern and Medieval Languages at Cambridge (including Linguistics under John Trim). He worked as a translator at the European Parliament from 1974 and became Director of Translation in 1990 and Director General of Translation and Publishing in 1995. In 2001 he was appointed Director General of Personnel.

*Proliferation = reproduce / exist in large numbers*

# *Introduction*

*pragmatic = concerned with practical results, reasons and values*

ARTURO TOSI

*freelancer = independant journalist, writer, etc who sells his service wherever he can*

In the past ten years the problems of translation in multilingual environments have attracted increasing attention both inside and outside Europe. The European Union (EU) has, of course, been the source and the sponsor of many such debates, because of its ambitious project to enable Europe to speak with one voice but in many languages.

Some of the discussions focus on technical issues, such as the powerful impact of modern technology on the speed and accuracy of translation; others debate political matters, lamenting the dominant role of some languages – such as French and increasingly English – which undermines the fundamental principles of the EU's multilingual policy. Other debates examine practical operations, including the attempt to maintain the commitment to full multilingualism despite an equally strong commitment to future enlargements, with the consequent proliferation of language combinations and the inevitable cost increases that these will bring.

The initiative of gathering together a mixed group of translators and language researchers to look at multilingual translation with a view to seeking consensus and identifying priorities for a way forward was welcomed by all translators from the EU Parliament who attended the conference in great numbers. The conference itself was a one-day event in November 1998 and the programme was designed with a view to mapping out and discussing the most relevant theoretical and pragmatic issues about multilingual translation. The structure of this book aims to reflect this dynamic interaction between the groups of discussants. Part 1 includes some academic overviews on multilingualism presented in the plenary session. Part 2 includes four papers that examine further aspects of the debate – the role of freelancers, information technology and the media. Finally, Part 3 reports on the Round Table that followed and the discussions from the three thematic workshops that were attended by translators from all the different language services.

Barry Wilson's paper opens this book with a survey of the issues surrounding <u>multilingual translation in the EU</u>, which includes the <u>historical,</u> <u>legal and political</u> aspects. He explains that the work of the Translation Service is essential to the functioning of the European Parliament but he also reminds us of the importance of the changes underway. The future admission of new Member States will create a complex system of combinations of language pairs for translation. It is predictable that the additional financial burden of maintaining full multilingualism in the EU will be politically more acceptable if the system can be fine-tuned to the satisfaction of all parties involved. This point indicates that the conference on multilingual translation came at a good point in time and also reminds us that no linguistic <u>panacea</u> has ever been found to solve translation problems. Indeed, as Barry Wilson concludes, safeguarding full multilingualism is important both politically and culturally and professional training in translation is an area worthy of investment, as it will always play a key role in the maintenance of the fundamental values of freedom of expression, freedom of information and respect for the cultural and human values of Europe.

[handwritten margin note: remedy for all troubles]

John Trim's paper does not specifically address the issue of professional awareness, though the author devotes much of his remarks to the <u>interpenetration of languages in contact</u>, which is often held to be a source of dilemma and anxiety among translators. Trim argues that interpenetration between languages and cultures in contact, mediated by plurilingual speakers, is not new. He points out that languages, whether in the multiculturalism of society or in the plurilingualism of the individual, do not simply exist side by side. They interact and interpenetrate one another. Plurilingual competence has always enabled language users to translate and interpret texts, and to introduce foreign words which, with frequent use, are adapted and integrated into the receiving language. Perhaps the question arises, he says, as to whether this process is an inevitable development, changing but enriching rather than impoverishing the languages concerned, or whether it is a threat to linguistic and cultural integrity, to be monitored, controlled and, where possible, resisted. In this sense, expressions which at first seem strange may come to be accepted as normal, especially if the language of origin holds a high level of prestige. <u>Trim</u> argues that <u>not even English can remain uncontaminated by international loan word traffic</u>, although he sees the process as beneficial. As for the escalating process of English becoming an international lingua franca, he considers the fear of those who see a danger to other cultures and an unfair advantage to English-speaking peoples, and who therefore look to political and educational measures to redress the imbalance. Trim's argument that negative administrative measures (like those adopted by some governments in Eastern Europe in the post-war period), would not be effective or acceptable in democratic societies was most welcome by translators. But it was his final conclusions that were met with most enthusiasm. He said that he felt very optimistic about the vitality of the 50 or more European national, or regional, languages – they encourage other Europeans to understand and participate in the life of the countries they come to know as a result of increasing educational and vocational mobility.

Chris Rollason's study of language contacts, involving French and English inside and outside the EU headquarters, reinforces Trim's point that no European language can exist in isolation, and that linguistic interaction with lexical interpenetration is a natural condition especially in a period of increased cultural globalisation. Of course, this evolution poses problems of choice for translators, who are suddenly confronted with a number of options. Some of these may be acceptable within the national community, while others may have mainly gained status and currency in EU specialist quarters, where French and English coexist as the two working languages and are used interchangeably by most staff. Rollason's paper is a stimulating study of the complexity of language interpenetration, which challenges the simple assumption that linguistic borrowings are the by-products of linguistic snobbery by monolingual speakers or of professional sloppiness by plurilingual translators. A researcher and translator himself, Rollason takes pleasure in demonstrating how contextual and intellectual conditions play an important role in determining lexical choices, which ultimately acquire currency and credibility within the speech community that generates them: sometimes they result from individual conformism, sometimes from group irony, often from both. Rollason's paper has deliberately been written in humorous tones in contrast to the widespread purism which often dominates popular, as well as academic, discussions defending cultural and linguistic integrity.

Renato Correia's paper shifts the focus of the discussion from issues of lexical choice to the problems of legal concepts in different languages. Here the dilemma is not merely one of puristic versus liberal lexical choices: the problem is that some national traditions have certain legal concepts, while others do not; and this effectively means that there can, at times, be no equivalence between translated legal texts. Correia revisits historically the concepts of drafting and translating within the Community: he points out that the difficulty of 'equivalent translation' did not arise in early European legislation, when texts were drafted jointly by multilingual teams of subject specialists. This practice has been abandoned and all European laws are now drafted in one language and then translated into the others. Indeed, Correia's point concerns the more general issue of cultural dominance in all EU documents, which is most evident in legal texts. Correia reminds us that whilst the highest standards of accuracy are expected in legal documents, these are difficult to attain since translators do not participate in the original drafting process. The author concludes that the whole approach needs to be reconsidered, since at present translators operate 'in a vacuum', not knowing whether the fundamental ambiguities in the legal texts have been deliberately made for political reasons or whether they are simply due to the limited linguistic competence of the writers who are not native-speakers of the language used to draft the texts.

TOST :   In my paper, I examine some of the issues and problems that emerged from these presentations, and I contend that the issues raised can be referred back to a 'translation culture' which was valid in the past, but is possibly no longer beneficial to the needs and priorities of the EU today. I therefore suggest that it would be useful to distinguish between minor difficulties – such as human imprecision or causes for puristic complaints – and institutional and structural problems that are more important from the point of view of communication and thus deserve further analysis and cross-linguistic comparison. For example, the 'myth' of multilingual equivalence highlighted by Correia seems to explain the in-house procedures and regulations that were established at the time of the Treaty of Rome in 1957. Their relevance today should be re-examined in the light of the new circumstances imposed by economic, legal and cultural globalisation. I conclude that the initiation of such research – beginning with the establishment of the linguistic observatory mentioned by John Trim – would help to distinguish which languages are more (or less) affected by the current approach, and that this should also tell us something about the reception of translations in Member States. For example, the two drafting languages – French and English – show similar linguistic trends when used in EU documents, and this sometimes results in calls for puristic campaigns at home. More serious problems of comprehensibility seem to affect the languages of those Europeans who are not native-speakers of the two drafting languages. Comprehensibility, of course, also depends on the level of standardisation of the national language, and I argue that the less a language is standardised the more it is penalised, as the impact of borrowings and neologisms creates more concern when it produces approximation rather than standardisation, for this can seriously limit the quality of communication as well as that of translation.

   Freddie De Corte's contribution advocates a higher esteem for the work of freelance translators, whose linguistic competence is often negatively contrasted with that of the permanent staff working within the Parliament. On the contrary, he argues that generalisations about linguistic competence and professional expertise at a time of global communication should take some important contextual circumstances into account. Freelance translators who live in their Member State and who are in contact with other native-speakers must, he says, be in a better position to make the right decisions than translators who operate within the EU Parliament and who are far from the everyday use of the target language. The controversy between freelancing versus in-house translators addresses only some parts of the problem of lexical choices and, in the long term, possibly not even the most important ones. All languages in Europe have evolved from within their cultural traditions and no national language is fully equipped to convey and communicate a new supranational European content. What has been said in other fields of applied linguistics research is thus true in the field of multilingual translation: that is, the native-speaker is dead. This is so because in a multilingual situation, when language contacts are the norm rather than the exception, the choices of the monolingual speaker can no longer serve to provide a universally reliable language model. What is new and important, in the new multilingual and intercultural reality of Europe, is the process of language standardisation that affects the voice of Europe; and this new use is emerging within the multilingual intercultural environment where all supranational decisions and operations take place, that is to say not in a national monolingual environment, but within a context of regular language contacts. This is a process worth examining and monitoring, and De Corte's paper stresses that it is important that all translators should be aware of it.

The next two following papers also deal with this process but from different standpoints. Both contributions examine the attempts to equip translation procedures with advanced information technology (IT) not only to increase production, but also with a view to consolidating new European terminologies and thus speeding up the standardisation of national languages when spoken in the common voice of Europe. Anne Tucker's paper is a comprehensive survey of two decades of collaboration between IT specialists and translators, which has improved both the quantity and the quality of translations, both in terms of speed and volume. Luca Tomasi's paper questions some of the IT applications – current and potential – vis-à-vis the problem of lexical and terminological standardisation, which affects communication and clarity, rather than from that of access to databases, which mainly benefits output and productivity. His paper on the central role of the translator in the identification of contextual collocations complements Anne Tucker's contribution and, at the same time, highlights a new and problematic issue on the current use of IT: whether European databases, which collect an enormous amount of lexical data in context, do or do not provide translators with the appropriate range of choices to narrow the gap between European use and national use of the language concerned.

The issue of translating European matters, with the clarity expected by European citizens living within their national communities, is taken up again in the paper by Christopher Cook. He starts by stressing the role of the media in educating citizens to develop a 'European-mindedness' and that of EU institutions in helping journalists to translate for their readers. The notion of the 'empty chair' that belongs to the audience, he said, should be a reminder that whether you are broadcasting or writing for a newspaper or a magazine whatever you say or write is practically worthless if no one hears or reads it.

The Workshop and Round Table reports should be of interest to readers as they clarify some of the views of different sectors of professionals present at the seminar: administrators, practitioners and users both outside and inside the EU Parliament. As a regular user of translations, a Swedish MEP, Malou Lindholm, stressed the greater accuracy and comprehensibility of texts, particularly legal texts, if they are translated in-house rather than externally by freelance translators, a point which was met with enthusiasm by all the staff translators present at the seminar. The need to rethink the present functioning and structure of the service, in the face of future enlargements and new combinations of languages, was stressed by both the Director of Interpretation of the EU Parliament and the Director-General of the EU Commission Translation Service. They also expressed the hope that a long-term policy for language education would be able to generate the interpretation and translation skills required by unusual 'pairs' of languages, since these human resources will be necessary to support the political commitment to full multilingualism. The translators themselves re-examined the issue of human and material resources vis-à-vis the standards of quality that are expected by the users of EU documents in all Member States. Some common views emerged, namely:

(a)  that it is perfectly clear to all the translators that an increasing number of European citizens today need to read EU materials;
(b)  that texts must be impeccable from the point of view of accuracy and of clarity; and
(c)  that translators today have a role as linguistic innovators in making the voice of Europe both heard and credible – a role that is sometimes misrepresented by the very concept of 'translator'.

This message which emerged from the Workshops and the Round Table, where the notion of the 'empty chair', representing the receiver's needs, was much quoted by the discussants, possibly as it was felt that it well summarised the challenges of multilingual translation for a United Europe: Is it really possible to have a single European voice? And to have it speak in different languages? I hope this book achieves, as much as the conference did, in making a positive contribution towards the consolidation of a new translation culture in support of European multilingualism.[1]

## Acknowledgements

I would like to express my gratitude to a number of people in the European Parliament who helped me with the planning of the book, contacts with the authors, and the collection and circulation of various papers before and after the conference. I am conscious of particular debt to Barry Wilson, Director-General of Translation and General Services at the European Parliament, for his encouragement throughout all the various phases of planning and execution of the project; to Delmira Astorri, Deputy Head of the Italian Translation Directorate, who was always at hand during the processes of organisation and consultation; to John Loydall, Head of the English Translation Directorate, for his indispensable guidance and advice; to Sergio Magri, Head of the Italian Translation Directorate, for his personal friendship and support. I would also like to thank all the translators who worked on the preparation of the Workshops and on the compilation of the subsequent reports: Sylvia Ball, Nichole Buchin, Renato Correia, Christopher Rollason, Edward Seymour and Helen Swallow. John Trim's readiness to advise on linguistic and European issues was much appreciated. I am very grateful to Freddie De Corte and Anne Tucker who went out of their way to meet my requirements, and to Christopher Cook and Luca Tomasi whose willingness to contribute to the project, though outsiders to the Translation Service of the European Parliament, gives this book a true sense of completeness. I would like to add that working with all these people was, for me, a most exciting and unforgettable experience.

## Note
1.  When this book was going to press I was made aware of a manuscript on European translation written by Emma Wagner to which the authors of the papers in this book were not able to refer. Of Emma Wagner's work we were already aware of the 'Fight the Fog' campaign, designed to promote clear writing among writers and translators.

## Chapter 1

# The Translation Service in the European Parliament

BARRY WILSON

In introducing these reflections on multilingualism as practised and perceived in the translation service of the European Parliament, I feel it may be helpful to give some background to illustrate the special multilingual context in which we work, how it came into being, what is its legal basis and how it functions in the daily life of the Institution.

The use of languages has been a frequent subject of debate in Parliament and it has reaffirmed its positions of principle in a number of reports which it has adopted on the subject, most recently the Decision of the European Parliament and the Council on the Establishment of 2001 as the European Year of Languages.

## Historical and Legal Aspects

The principle of equal status for the languages of the Member States was applied when the Union was established. Strikingly, no mention is made of the language issue in the ECSC Treaty of 25 July 1952 setting up the European Coal and Steel Community (ESSC). However, shortly before the entry into force of the ECSC Treaty, the Foreign Ministers of the six original Member States adopted a protocol in which it was agreed that French, German, Italian and Dutch were both the official languages and the working languages of the Community.

On 15 April 1958 the Council adopted Regulation No. 1 determining the languages to be used by the European Economic Community. Article 1 of this Regulation states: 'The official languages and the working languages of the institutions of the Community shall be Dutch, French, German and Italian.'

Thus, by a unanimous vote, the Council institutionalised in the EEC and the European Atomic Energy Community the full multilingualism introduced within the framework of the ECSC.

The Council conclusions of 12 June 1995 on linguistic diversity and multilingualism in the European Union (EU) emphasised that 'linguistic diversity must be preserved and multilingualism promoted in the Union, with equal respect for the languages of the Union and with due regard to the principle of subsidiarity'.

Parliament has argued in a number of its resolutions in favour of retaining the system of using several languages. The Nyborg report, for instance, emphasises the use of the Union's official languages on an equal footing at all meetings of Parliament and its bodies (with interpreting both into and from all languages and use of all languages in both speech and writing).

The Hänsch report on European Union also states that the languages of the Member States of the EU are the Union's official languages. All citizens and representatives are entitled to speak their own language within the institutions of the Union and to request information about the policies and workings of the Union in that language. They also receive information in their own language.

The Maastricht Treaty also encourages the use of the various languages. Language, after all, is an essential aspect of individual cultures and, according to Article 128 of the Treaty, 'the Community shall contribute to the flowering of the cultures of the Member States'.

Parliament's own arrangements as regards language use are laid down in Rule 117 of its Rules of Procedure:

(1) All documents of Parliament shall be drawn up in the official languages.
(2) Speeches delivered in one of the official languages shall be simultaneously interpreted into the other official languages and into any other language the Bureau may consider necessary.

## Political Aspects

Linguistic and cultural diversity are really what gives the EU its specific character, distinguishing it from other large trading partners such as the United States. This diversity is sometimes felt as a hindrance to free movement within the EU, one of the fundamental rights which underpin the Union, because citizens are much more reluctant to seek work in another Member State whose language they do not understand or whose way of life is uncongenial to them. Harmonisation of social security provisions and mutual recognition of diplomas have helped but there has been a relative lack of flexibility in the labour market, although there have been some significant movements of migrant workers.

On the other hand the immense intellectual capital and creativity to which Europe's rich history and cultural diversity give rise are a great advantage in a rapidly changing world where innovation provides a real competitive edge.

Parliamentary representatives at European level reflect this cultural diversity. It is therefore only right and proper that Parliament should use all of the Member States' languages in its work.

Another argument for full multilingualism put forward in the Galle report of 1994 on the right to use one's own language is that Members (MEPs) should speak their own language in European debate because they are not in the European Parliament to represent themselves but to represent their electorate.

The first requirement to be able to represent the electorate properly is, literally, to speak their language. This also makes the Member's work directly accessible to European citizens and enables them to understand and monitor the work of the Members elected by them. Any limitations on the number of languages used would infringe this principle to a considerable degree and fail to respect voters' right to be represented.

The report goes on to stress that the obligation to use a language other than one's own for parliamentary work is tantamount to a language knowledge requirement. Such an obligation would be undemocratic, if only because it would mean that access to Parliament would not be universal. In other words, such a rule would be an eligibility requirement which would not apply to all EU nationals. It would mean introducing distinctions on the basis of knowledge of languages – in an arena where Parliament champions equality for all in a large number of fields.

The political sensitivity of this issue cannot be overemphasised. A recent proposal to change the method of drafting daily press briefings directly in 11 languages to one where they were drafted in one language and then translated two hours later produced an outcry in Spain where it was presented as relegating Spanish (and the other languages) to second-class status.

## Multilingualism in Practice

### For translators

Altogether in the Institutions of the Union more than 3000 translators are employed and they produce over 2 million translated pages every year. In the European Parliament 500 translators organised in 11 language divisions produce 700,000 translated pages a year. We have no statistics indicating how many of these pages are read a year. We sincerely hope that many are and, in fact, we believe this to be the case because on four or five occasions each year MEPs take the trouble to point out to us the occasional mistake which creeps in to this substantial volume of work.

To give some notion of the volumes, every day each translation division receives around 300 pages to translate, the equivalent of translating a novel into ten different languages every working day. The source languages are more evenly spread than in any other institution as any MEP can table an amendment, resolution or parliamentary question in his or her own language and has the right to have it reproduced in all the languages of the Union. The deadlines are usually very short, ranging from a few days for committee work down to 2 hours during parliamentary sessions. This requires us to provide 24 hour coverage of 110 language combinations at a high level of skill and quality.

To provide these skills translators are recruited by public competitive examination. A university degree in any subject together with university-level knowledge of at least two languages of the Union is a basic require-ment. However, it takes some years to reach the level of experience and competence required to translate sensitive political speeches or complex legislation under the co-decision procedure.

### For MEPs

Many MEPs who are able to speak several languages take the view that in an institution where all working languages enjoy equal status, switching to another language is a mistaken concession to colleagues with a different native language. The explanatory statement to the Galle report of 1994 put it like this:

> Anyone who has taken the trouble to learn a foreign language knows that genuine multilingualism is a rare phenomenon. Most of us have full mastery of our mother tongue only. Clearly, those allowed to speak their own language are in a *politically* stronger position. Being allowed to speak your own language is an advantage over those who are obliged to muddle along as best they can in another language. Con-versely, those who are not allowed to speak their own language have handed over a *weapon* to political opponents with a different mother tongue.

In spite of this radical position, it is an illusion to imagine that every form of written and spoken communication in the European Parliament passes through the voices or pens of our interpreters and translators. Much informal direct communication occurs and of course the institution would not function without it. Members do not walk the corridors shadowed by

an interpreter. Nor is every note and letter they write passed to an amanu-
ensis to convey it in the other 10 tongues of the Union.

In the meeting rooms they do depend on the high-level language skills of
their interpreters to convey their cogent advocacy of their points of view
and they certainly need the painstakingly accurate translations of the draft
legislation and amendments on which they are to vote. But outside those
rooms MEPs do communicate with each other face to face in their political
groups or in informal discussions. Indeed they actively pursue their study
of languages to make sure this communication is possible. Nearly half of
the MEPs are studying a language and many more express themselves
fluently in one or more foreign languages.

Some European politicians take the view that they wish their message to
be understood as directly as possible by as large a number of listeners as
possible rather than have it mediated through the voices of interpreters.
The European Ombudsman, a Swedish-speaking Finn, and the President
of the European Central Bank, a Dutch speaker, choose to address the
European Parliament in English. The President of the Commission, Mr
Prodi, was recently embarrassed in the European Parliament when
attempting to deliver his speech in Italian, as the Italian translation of his
English original was delivered to him only moments before he started
speaking.

The existence of these direct forms of communication through languages which are spoken and understood at various levels certainly has an
influence on the development of those languages, at least in our own
special political context. It is likely that such effects on the languages filter
through, perhaps through the press, to the wider European public. This
aspect was also dealt with in our seminar.

Paradoxically, the translation and interpreting services strive, in the
areas where their skills are brought into play, to stop this happening. Our
aim is to isolate languages. It is to maintain a fiction that each MEP exists
and works in a monolingual environment or at least to simulate such an
environment. If this policy were taken to its logical conclusion, and if
there were enough money available, every word MEPs hear and read
would be in their own language. Like the boy in the bubble they would be
protected from any contamination (except that in this case it is the interpreters who sit in the bubbles, the glass-fronted booths in the meeting
rooms).

Of course, while political lip service is paid to this fiction, the reality is
that MEPs work in a small linguistic melting pot in which terms from
foreign languages acquire a specific meaning for them. Sometimes when
they read the term in their own language they find it difficult to under-

stand. Unfortunately when the public hear this alien language they condemn it as impenetrable jargon.

## The Costs Now and in the Future

We are looking forward now to a Europe of 27 Member States and 22 languages. Of course costs will increase as new languages are added and both the translation and interpretation services are studying technical ways of dealing with this enlargement in such a way as to provide the full respect for the right for MEPs to use their own language, while limiting those costs. Solutions such as relay translation through a pivot language, interpretation from outside the meeting room using audio-visual links and control over which texts must be produced in all languages, based on real needs, are being explored.

Questions are being raised, however, in the Budgets Committee about more radical steps including more use of the private sector (already 28% of the translation work in Parliament is contracted out and more than half the interpreters used are freelance) and possible devolution to the Member States of some of the work and costs of translation.

However, restrictions on translation and interpreting into certain languages would not necessarily lead to savings, but rather to a shift in translation costs from the European level to the national or regional level. If Parliament were, for instance, to decide to restrict the number of working languages used during parliamentary proceedings and to translate only the final result into all the languages concerned, the various interim stages (working documents, draft reports, amendments and so on) would nonetheless have to be translated – but at the expense of the MEP concerned or his or her party, for the benefit of his or her own electorate. Apart from the fact that this would lead to indirect discrimination between MEPs, it would also entail the risk of disparate, non-uniform terminology, whereas the development of European terminology in all languages is one of the advantages of the existing system. If we went further and devolved the translation of legislation to the Member States, differing interpretations might be introduced at national level, giving rise to distortions in the application of EU legislation from one state to another.

However, the costs entailed by the current language system actually account for only a modest part of the administrative costs of the EU. Even after the accession of Finland and Sweden, the costs of translation and interpreting did not increase significantly as a proportion of total running costs. It should also be realised that the EU's operational budget as a whole is still extremely modest, representing less than 5% of EU expenditure. Even on the broadest interpretation, language costs are not more than a quarter of that sum and therefore only just over 1% of the costs of running the EU.

This is surely a price worth paying to safeguard the fundamental values of freedom of expression, freedom of information and respect for the cultural and human values of the European continent.

## Chapter 2

# Multilingualism and the Interpretation of Languages in Contact

JOHN TRIM

I should first like to thank the organisers of this seminar for inviting me to introduce the theme of the seminar. I should also like to thank you for allowing me to speak in my own mother tongue. Your willingness to do so is evidence of your own advanced plurilingualism. There can be no doubt that for those who speak only their mother tongue, the division of Europe into so many distinct language groups erects a virtually insuperable barrier to communication. However, for those who have achieved an effective knowledge of other languages, variety is a source of great mutual enrichment. Perhaps it may help to resolve the paradox posed by the title of our seminar to distinguish between societal *multilingualism,* the existence of more than one language community in a society, which places a barrier to communication between the communities concerned, and individual *plurilingualism,* the ability of the individual to communicate through more than one language, which builds bridges between them. Plurilinguals are, by their essence, bridge-builders and as professional translators you are, of course, the most accomplished.

It may also be useful to place translation in a more general frame of language activities. The Common European Framework for language learning, teaching and assessment (CEF) which has been developed by the Council of Europe with support from the European Union (EU) divides language activities into production, reception, interaction and mediation (Council of Europe, 2001). By 'production' we mean the production of a spoken or written text, presented to a listener or reader in a one-way process which the recipient cannot affect – what I was doing in my study when preparing this paper and am doing now when delivering it. You, on the other hand, are involved in a purely receptive activity as listeners now and perhaps as readers once the text is published. Interaction, as in conversation, negotiation, discussion and debate, is not simply a succession of acts of production and reception by each partner in turn. It is a joint activity which involves the participants in negotiating meanings and producing a common understanding. Later they may find it hard to recall exactly who said what. They are obliged to listen and plan ahead at the same time. Intensified European cooperation, understanding and mobility make it necessary for all young Europeans to learn to use foreign languages in all these ways. The recent Eurobarometer on young people facing the Millennium shows that a majority of Europe's under-twenty-fives now feel confident in their competence to communicate in at least one language other than their mother tongue and are motivated to learn more (European Commission, 1997). Those who are unable to communicate with each other directly must have recourse to mediation.

We speak of mediation when a person uses his or her knowledge of languages not to express his or her own ideas but rather to bridge between others who are unable to understand each other and to communicate directly. This can happen within the limits of a single language, where one party uses a specialised technical language unintelligible to the partner. More commonly, bridging is required across languages. Anyone with any knowledge of a foreign language may be called upon to provide this service for others who have none – and we should remember that if two-thirds of young people in Europe have a conversational competence in at least one foreign language, one-third have none and that language skills are much less widespread among the middle-aged and the elderly (Eurydice, 1997).

In any case, the growing ability of young people to communicate directly by means of languages other than their mother tongue does not reduce the need for high-quality professional translation and interpretation. Admittedly, most people will prefer to deal directly with the business of daily living themselves and to make human contacts face to face. However, when it comes to important matters with serious long-term consequences, demanding precision and sensitivity, they will prefer to use the full resources of their mother tongue and pass a carefully formulated text to a competent translator – or, receptively, to rely on a competent translator or interpreter rather than on their own limited linguistic ability. Indeed, the intensification of international communication can only mean a large and continuing demand for translation services, particularly since we cannot expect the general run of busy people to find the time and energy to learn more than two or three of the 50 or more national and recognised regional languages in Europe, let alone the major languages of Asia and Africa. The problem may rather be to manage the demand, say by giving serious attention to computer-assisted translation and to other ways of using information technology (IT) to assist independent access to documentation in a wide range of languages.

While both translators and interpreters are engaged in mediation, the two activities differ greatly, largely because of the differing nature and functions of spoken and written language. Spoken language is a universal activity of human beings. All human beings, whether intelligent or not, seem able to learn words and combine them in a systematic way into an indefinite number of sentences which members of the same language community can understand without having previously encountered them. They acquire this ability without formal learning, simply as a result of socialisation in the context of continual exposure to the language spoken around them (Chomsky, 1965). When explorers have encountered new human communities in inaccessible places the question is not 'Do they have a language?' but rather 'What is their language like?' Experience shows that the structure of the languages of communities in an early stage of technological development is, if anything, of greater formal complexity than that of the technologically advanced. Writing, on the other hand, is by no means universal. Human society developed over untold thousands of years without, so far as we know, any use of a permanent representation of language. They had to rely on the extraordinary feats of memory of which pre-literate people appear to be capable.

The processes of speech communication are perhaps the most demanding tasks which human beings face (Fry, 1977). A speaker has to convert a multidimensional complex of ideas into linear form using the grammar and lexicon of the language and observing the sociocultural conventions which govern their use, and then organise the rapid, highly skilled movements of the organs of speech so as to produce the sound waves which convey the necessary information to the listener. The listener must then perceive the words and sentences being transmitted (Denes & Pinson, 1993). Their structure has to be identified and meanings have to be ascribed and interpreted in the verbal and situational context. All this has to be done in real time. The process is only possible if the participants share a complex of competences built up in their previous experience and even then places very heavy demands on human processing capacities and on memory. As a result conversations are marked by high redundancy, frequent performance errors, hesitations, false starts and self-correction. Its success depends upon the extent to which the partners share a common background and goodwill.

Written communication has different characteristics. It develops later both in the individual and in the community. A written text is a spatial artefact. Once produced it remains in existence until it is physically destroyed. It enables both writer and reader to communicate across space and time. It is by no means universal but has to be learnt by a conscious effort on the basis of the prior acquisition and in fact analysis of the spoken language. Its role in the life of the individual and of society is much more limited but more conscious and controlled. However, it has some advantages. The writer is not forced, as is the case in speech, to produce a linear sequence of symbols in real time, but has time for reflection, formulation, error correction and revision of which the reader may be unaware. The reader is confronted only with the finished product and does not have to deal with it in real time. It is much easier for both writers and readers to think and look ahead and refer back, to take in chunks at a time, to pick out key words and reflect upon meaning in ways which, in spoken language, would be either impossible or make heavy calls on memory and prediction.

Whilst language as such is universal among human beings and is used by them all for rather similar purposes in rather similar ways (how else would translation be possible?), particular language systems vary enormously. The most basic ground rules of grammar seem to be universal but all surface features appear to be arbitrary and rest upon usage which is in continual flux. No two people acquire language in precisely the same form. Innovations creep into a community and spread unequally, whilst other features go out of fashion, out of use and are forgotten. When speakers of a language spread out over a wide area and live local lives and lose touch, their speech diversifies, a 'rainbow' of dialects results and mutual intelligibility across the whole area is lost. Over the long expansion of the human species, a huge number of mutually unintelligible languages have come into existence. Crystal (1987) speaks of some 4000 distinct languages in the world. Most are spoken by small communities and it seems most likely that there are a much larger number which are extinct. In historical times we have seen this process at work as a result of the collapse of the Roman Empire and the great migrations now more than 1500 years ago. As to pre-history, we can use methods of comparative linguistics to reconstruct hypothetical source languages for clearly related families of languages such as the Indo-European, the Finno-Ugrian and the Semitic, but in view of the immense antiquity of the human race these methods will give us access only to its most recent developments. Where we can look at societies which may still resemble those of an earlier epoch, they are characterised by extreme diversity, perhaps because the only peoples to have remained in that condition are small communities, living in mountainous or afforested areas where communications are difficult. Areas such as the Amazonian rain-forest or the Central Highlands of New Guinea are extremely multilingual. The multiplicity of mutually incomprehensible languages reflects and reinforces the barriers to communication imposed by the terrain. Even so, bridges are necessary to communicate with their nearest neighbours. People need to learn a second language, even though relations may be restricted to war, cannibalism and exogamy. Wherever conditions allow, men are highly mobile. The world is criss-crossed by ancient trade routes and history starts as a record of continual movement; trade, conquest, migration and wandering. These movements of individuals and of whole communities form a kaleidoscope of shifting relations, always bringing peoples and languages into contact and mutual influence, effected by the plurilingualism of individuals. Scholars have shown, in considerable detail, how ancient political boundaries leave their mark and how linguistic and cultural innovations spread, wave-like, along the arteries of communication (Bloomfield, 1933). Influences, though to some extent mutual, are rarely symmetrical. The immigrant takes much more from the host community than majority populations take from minorities, unless the minority are conquerors or in possession of material or cultural products that the majority feel they need. In this case, a whole population may become bilingual, leading perhaps to the total abandonment of their original language, as we can see in the case of the Romanised Celts in NW mainland Europe (though not of the offshore islands). However, the influence of the original mother tongue may still be present as a substrate influence through the interference of the mother tongue in the learning of the dominant language as a second language during the bilingual period. Otherwise, contact with members of an alien community who contribute something new and valuable to the development of a society will normally lead to the adoption not only of the cultural artefacts and concepts but also of the corresponding words and even grammatical devices.

Multilingualism, and plurilingualism in response to it, is probably the normal condition of mankind. Of course, if there is little need for communication across language boundaries, most people can live their lives as unilinguals in a monolingual environment, leaving outside communication to those directly engaged in cross-border activities and to a relatively small class of professional plurilingual intermediaries. Otherwise, a degree of plurilingualism may mark a cultural and intellectual élite. Ethnic minority communities as well as individual immigrants and refugees are expected to become plurilingual and to communicate with the majority in their language. In such unequal communication situations there is little or no pressure upon the majority population to concern itself with the language of the minority. This was, to a large extent, the linguistic profile of many European nation states until recently. Since the Second World War, however, the rapid development of communications and information technologies has transformed societies across the world. No sector of European society is exempt from the effects of economic, political, social and cultural globalisation. Plurilingualism is now a mass requirement and is already on the way to becoming universal in the younger generation. As a result of the operation of a self-reinforcing spiral, a combination of powerful forces has, perhaps irreversibly, made English the principal medium of international communication in many fields on a global scale, without however weakening the vitality of the internal use of the 50 or so European national and regional languages large and small. Europe is and will remain multilingual and plurilingualism cannot limit itself to mother tongue plus English. Educational and occupational mobility as well as the need for mutuality in international understanding and cooperation mean that individuals will need to expand their linguistic repertoire throughout life in order to move with freedom and effectiveness within the multilingual and multicultural reality of Europe.

Neither in the multiculturalism of society nor the plurilingualism of the individual do languages simply exist side by side. They interact and interpenetrate. The plurilingual competence of language users is more than the sum of its parts. It enables them to translate and interpret, to mediate between unilinguals, to codeswitch as ideas come more easily in one language than another, bringing foreign words into a discourse which with frequent use become adapted and integrated into the receiving language. Thus words from Latin and Greek, perhaps directly, perhaps via a third language, have entered most modern European languages in modified forms. They are, nevertheless, generally recognisable in a foreign language and greatly reduce the effort needed to construct the meaning of texts in a familiar field. Indeed, as a result of this international loan-word traffic we all have some plurilingual competence simply from our mother tongues. As a result of the cultural convergence produced by – especially literary – translation, direct interpersonal communication is made progressively easier.

However, when words of foreign origin enter a language, they do not always have the same meaning as in the language of origin. In French, *shopping* and *parking* are places, not actions. In English, *cul-de-sac* is used where the French say *impasse*, a word used in English to speak of a moment in a negotiation when neither side will compromise to reach a solution. In the course of time, the meanings of cognate words in different languages diverge. Thus in English, *realise* has largely lost its meaning 'to convert into reality' and is mainly used in the sense of 'to become aware of the true situation'. *Model* is no longer something of excellence to be copied, but rather a schema which can be used by others as a basis for their independent reflection and manipulation ('there are a number of models of grammar for teachers to draw on') or even a particular type of product ('Chrysler have brought out a new model'). The meaning of these words is thus different from *réaliser* and *modèle* in French, or *realisieren* and *Modell* in German. Similarly *sympathetic* is not equivalent to *sympa(thique)* or *sympathisch*. Such mismatches are well known as *faux amis*. Of course, false friends can only deceive if they resemble the great mass of true friends! Most often the cognate is usable and under pressure of time simultaneous interpreters may come to use cognates without reflection and so may translators if there is a mass of material to process to an imminent deadline. This applies not only to individual words but also to idioms and even grammatical constructions. There is a great temptation to follow them word for word unless the result is clearly ridiculous. If this practice is carried out over a long period, expressions which at first seem strange may come to be accepted as normal – especially if the language of origin has a high prestige. This was long the case with Latin, which has left its imprint not only on the Romance languages, but also on the syntax of Germanic languages and their received stock of formulaic expressions. From the 17th century to the 19th, French played something of the same role. In the EU at present English and French, as the principal drafting languages, exert a similar pressure on others, especially perhaps those of less populous Member States. Furthermore, the increasingly dominant role of English in many aspects of international and even national life is producing an even heavier pressure upon all other languages. As we have seen, the process of interpenetration among languages and cultures in contact, mediated by plurilinguals, is by no means new. The question arises as to whether this process is an inevitable development, changing but enriching rather than impoverishing the languages concerned or whether it is a threat to their linguistic and cultural integrity, to be monitored, controlled and, where possible, resisted.

It may perhaps shed some light on this issue if we look briefly at a case in which a European language has been subject to the massive impact of outside influences, namely English itself.

The various settlers who came across the North Sea – Angles, Saxons and Jutes (or perhaps Frisians) – appear to have taken little or nothing beyond a few place names from the British they displaced or, in some cases, assimilated but brought with them the words earlier generations had taken from the Romans, words concerned with construction, clothing and the growing and preparation of food as well as some terms from commerce and administration. The language was probably differentiated into distinct but, on the whole, mutually intelligible dialects from the start, with variety increased by North Germanic influences during the Danish hegemony, with some semantic differentiation of phonetically distinct synonyms, e.g. the distinction of skirt (Norse) from shirt (Anglo-Saxon) and dyke from ditch. The 'semi-communication' between Danes and Anglo-Saxons living in close proximity to each other is credited with the gradual emergence of a language drawing elements from both and shedding its inherited morphological complexity along the way: a change in the spoken language not overt in written forms until later.

A further dimension to Old English was added by the conversion of the island to Christianity, especially in its Roman form. From AD597 onward, cultural life was dominated by clerics who were bilingual in their mother tongue (not necessarily English) and Latin and who studied and wrote primarily in Latin. It was Alfred the Great who insisted on the translation of key texts into English.

> It seems better to me that we should translate certain books which are most necessary for all men to know, into the language which we can all understand and also arrange it so that all the youth of free men now among the English people are able to read English writing as well.

Here, he was following the example of Charlemagne in attempting to use a common language as a national unifying factor.

The Norman Conquest introduced a form of multilingualism typical of colonialism. The language of the court and the nobility was French. That of the church and of intellectual life was Latin. English was reduced to a *patois* of the common people, virtually unrepresented in written documents. The deeply divisive effects have been felt ever since. In fact, the use of French as the official court language lasted for some 350 years, but long before that it was, like Latin, more a learnt than a first language even for the minor nobility. McCrum *et al.* (1992) quote William of Bessyngton writing as early as 1325:

> Latin can noone speak, I trow
> But those who it from school do know;
> And some know French and no Latin
> Who're used to court and dwell therein,
> And some use Latin, though in part
> Who if known have not the art,
> And some can understand English
> That neither Latin know nor French
> But simple or learned, old or young
> All understand the English tongue.

In fact, at what appeared to be the time of greatest humiliation and degradation for the English language the conditions were being created for perhaps its greatest flowering. In the late Middle Ages, as the dominance of French faded and the emergent middle class grew in self-confidence, Middle English was enriched by a huge influx of loan-words from (Norman) French and from Latin and with a more developed syntax based on Latin models. In the 16th century the process was accelerated by the revival of learning in the Renaissance and by the Reformation, in which the translation of the Bible and a literacy drive to place it in the hands of ordinary people played a central role.

In the early modern period, the voyages of discovery ended the encapsulation of Europe and opened up the entire globe to exploration and trade, bringing a knowledge of the natural world and of a wide range of alternative cultures to Europe. Whereas in the Middle Ages scholars were hard put to it to find 72 languages for the post-Babel condition, by the 17th and 18th centuries they had to link languages into families to keep the number down! The huge growth of scientific terminology using Latin and Greek elements led to a great expansion of the vocabulary of English, since the mechanisms for anglicising words of classical origin were already in place.

Early on, English maritime technology derived much of its knowledge and terminology from Dutch and Portuguese. In the 18th and 19th centuries the industrial revolution and the dominance of sea-lanes gave Britain a world outlook, global trade links, imperial responsibilities and a global diaspora. One result was a great importation of words of the most diverse provenance for plants and animals as well as for exotic artefacts and cultural phenomena. At the same time English began to be used as a global trade language. In the present century that function has extended for a variety of reasons to other areas of international life, especially with the seamless transfer of British power to the United States during and after the Second World War.

I think you will agree, from this brief survey, that the development of the English language has resulted from the repeated impact of other languages and cultures as a result of varying kinds of multilingualism, mediated through plurilingual individuals. The process has, in my view, been entirely beneficial, particularly in the following respects:

(1)  The formal structure of the language has been greatly simplified, with the relations among the elements of the sentence shown by syntax rather than morphology.
(2)  A very rich lexicon has developed, with near-synonyms providing for differences of register and connotation.
(3)  English has been polycentric from the start. However, the phenomena of globalisation and the revolution in communication and information technology mean that the English-speaking countries interact and their languages converge as much as they diverge: Thus recent developments in British English result not only from changes in internal class and gender relations, but also from Australian and, particularly, American influences communicated especially via entertainment media. An intonation which in 1980 I found being discussed by Australians as an invasive feature of Queensland women's speech is now in

common use among young people in the UK. 'My home is in – Mansfield?' requires confirmation, not of its truth, but that Mansfield is known to the listener and needs no further explanation. As to US influence, an English woman could no longer reply to an American visitor asking 'Do you have children?' 'No, I'm 45 and I've got two already.'

(4) The English attitude to language is open to innovation, seeing diversity and change as enrichment rather than corruption.

(5) These developments have increased its accessibility especially to beginners. The co-existence of roughly synonymous words of Anglo-Saxon, Romance and classical origin means that learners of many European languages will find a fair proportion of words familiar especially for reading.

It seems ironic, but is perhaps appropriate, that the language which has absorbed more than any other from other languages and has been transformed by the process, should now have emerged as the prime medium of global communication. Nothing succeeds like success. Increasing international use and an increasingly firm place as the first (often the only) foreign language in schools in many parts of the world, together form an ascending, mutually reinforcing, spiral. It is already becoming difficult to deliver a plenary address to a World Congress (even of linguists) in a language other than English. Scientists and scholars wishing to reach a global audience increasingly feel that they must publish in English. Some people are alarmed by this escalating process, seeing a danger to other cultures and an unfair advantage to English-speaking peoples, even the threat of an Anglo-Saxon hegemony. They look to political and educational measures to reduce the imbalance.

Personally, I rather doubt whether administrative measures of a negative character, like those adopted by some governments in Eastern Europe in the post-war period, would be effective or acceptable in democratic societies. I do believe that positive measures should be taken to encourage a greater degree of plurilingualism, motivating young people (and older ones) to explore the multilingual and multicultural reality of Europe and other parts of the world. I have written elsewhere (Trim, 1999) of what I see as the disadvantages for native English-speakers of the leading international role of English – there is little evidence, I fear, that the political and economic influence of the United Kingdom is at an all-time high! Overall, I feel very optimistic about the vitality of the 50 or more European national and regional languages in the lives of the people who speak and write them. I am confident that this vitality will make other Europeans want to understand and enter into the life of the countries that they get to know as a result of increasing educational and vocational mobility. I do not think they will long be satisfied with trying to do so only through the medium of an international lingua franca. But then, one of the disadvantages I spoke of in being a native speaker of English is that I cannot expect you to be surprised or impressed let alone convinced, by my *insouciance* at the spread of its use!

Be that as it may, the international role of English raises issues for translators of a kind that may differ in a number of ways from those which face colleagues working with other languages (other perhaps than French). The initiators of an English language text for translation may well not be native speakers. This means for one thing that the background of cultural assumptions and rhetorical conventions will not be those of the UK or Ireland (which are themselves diverse according to regional and social class provenance). These differences have to be understood, but presumably respected in accordance with the fundamental criterion of fidelity. There may also be deviations from normal English grammar. If a German-speaking colleague, for instance, writes 'We are in Kosovo for a long time now' the translator must hope to be able to tell from the context whether he is writing of the present and recent past or of the future. In British usage it would of course be forward-looking. Problems may also arise with regard to idiom. Spoken English is highly idiomatic. A written text which is a transcript of a spontaneous speech will contain many idiomatic expressions, often in an abbreviated form or, especially in the case of proverbs, merely alluded to and quite often opaque, e.g. 'That's the last straw' or 'it's a wise child' – meaning that the origin of a proposal is obscure. The translator has not only to understand the idiom and recognise allusions but also to decide – as always under severe time pressure – whether to translate the idiom itself, which may or may not exist in the target language, or to find a target language equivalent, in accordance with the more problematic criterion of equivalence of effect or to abandon the idiom and express the idea in plain language, losing the stylistic value of the idiom. Each solution has its gains, losses and dangers. The task is even more problematic if a non-native speaker uses an idiom literally translated from his own language.

There is also of course the question of lexical deviation. We are all in danger from 'false friends'. If a non-native uses the word 'eventually' does s/he mean it in the usual native sense of 'finally, after a long time' or in the sense of 'if conditions are right'? In a political context, the distinction can be of importance, as can the inappropriate use of 'pretend' and 'deceive'. I am sure that as translators you are well aware of the traps and watch out for them but obviously the wider the range of background and levels of competence the writers of texts have, the more judgement is required from the hard-pressed translator.

The various pressures must, I am sure, tempt both writers and translators to fall back on routines to simplify the work. I recall well how often, during my work for the Council of Europe, Antonietta de Vigili would query a piece of English I particularly relished by asking: 'How would that translate into French?' Each translation produces a text which, for better or worse, then forms part of the corpus of that language and influences the subsequent use of the language, particularly by non-native speakers. Work pressures combined with a narrow interpretation of fidelity mean that translators will tend to keep as close as possible to the form of the original, departing from it only where the result would otherwise be unacceptable. The result may well be a convergence of texts over a period of time, especially in the case of French and English as the most frequently employed working languages of the international organisations. For English, that would be likely to mean a greater use of Romance elements in the lexicon and some loss of the immediacy and plasticity of the Anglo-Saxon – for instance preferring to tolerate something rather than just put up with it. Would the entirely understandable development of a bureau-cratic 'Eurospeak' be a good thing, facilitating and simplifying international communication and cooperation or an unacceptable impov-erishment of the languages concerned? On the face of it, perhaps, the former, provided that we are speaking simply of a special use of language for a defined, limited purpose. The full language is still there developing across the full range of its use, enriched by innumerable acts of creativity. However, given the power of news media, could Eurospeak be kept chained up, confined to use by the bureaucracy? Might it not escape to pollute the environment? Such fears bear more than a superficial similar-ity to those expressed by the opponents of genetic modification in the biological sphere!

Given that we can avoid a catastrophic collapse of our advanced techno-logical civilisation, with a breakdown of communication and the loss of contact that occurred in much of Europe 1500 years ago, I regard it as inevi-table that we as peoples, with our cultures and languages, will be in closer and closer touch with each other and will influence each other more and more. As professional translators you have a privileged position to see the process in action, to understand it, to contribute to it and report upon it. In return, I am sure that the effects of such observation and reflection on the quality of your work will be most beneficial. I trust that this seminar will be the first step in a programme of scientific and practical cooperation.

## References
Bloomfield, L. (1933) *Language*. London, Allen and Unwin.
Chomsky, N. (1965) *Aspects of the Theory of Syntax*. Cambridge, MA: MIT.

Council of Europe (1996) *A Common European Framework of Reference: Learning, Teaching, Assessment.* Cambridge: Cambridge University Press.

Crystal, D. (ed.) (1987) *The Cambridge Encyclopedia of Language.* Cambridge: Cambridge University Press.

Denes, P.B. and Pinson, E.N. (1993) *The Speech Chain: The Physics and Biology of Spoken Language,* 2nd edn. New York: Freeman.

European Commission (1997) *The Young Europeans: Eurobarometer 47.2.* Brussels: DG22, European Commission mimeograph.

Eurydice (1997) *Key Data on Education in the European Union.* Luxembourg : EU.

Fry, D.B. (1977) *Homo Loquens.* Cambridge: Cambridge University Press.

McCrum, R., Cran, W. and McNeil, R. (1992) *The Story of English,* 2nd revised edn. London: Faber & Faber and BBC.

Trim, J.L.M. (1999) Language education policies for the 21st century. In A. Tosi and C. Leung (eds) *Rethinking Language Education: From a Monolingual to a Multilingual Perspective.* London: Centre for Information on Language Teaching.

## Chapter 3

# The Use of Anglicisms in Contemporary French

CHRISTOPHER ROLLASON

## Contemporary French Writing and the Phenomenon of Anglicisms

Anglicisms and pseudo-anglicisms are scarcely a new phenomenon in French, as such long-established usages as 'le dandy' and 'le smoking' (for 'dinner-jacket') attest. A degree of cross-linguistic contamination has always been inevitable between such close neighbours (or 'frères ennemis') as Britain and France and, until relatively recently, the process has been a two-way one, with French enriching English with such usages as 'laissez-passer', 'maître d'hôtel' or, within living memory, 'cinéma-vérité' and 'nouvelle cuisine' – not to mention pseudo-gallicisms such as 'duvet' (for the object known in French as a 'couette'). In the last few decades, however, the question has taken on what is clearly a different dimension, as the prime source of anglicisms in French – as in all other languages – is no longer Britain, a country with approximately the same population and political and economic weight as France, but the United States, since 1989 the planet's sole hegemonic power. The issue of anglicisms now appears in France as an aspect of a much broader problem, namely the identity of Europe and its defence against perceived US domination in the economic, political and cultural fields.

Hostility to Americanisation is one of the recurrent themes in contemporary French journalism and polemical writing and is a position to be found on both sides of the left–right divide. The charges typically laid at the door of the United States by French intellectuals include, in particular, free-market evangelism, censorious neo-puritanism and mass-cultural domination. A number of examples of this tendency in France will now be quoted

The journalist Ignacio Ramonet, editor-in-chief of *Le Monde Diplomatique*, writes:

Les États-Unis (premiers producteurs de technologies nouvelles et siège des principales firmes) ont, à la faveur de la mondialisation de l'économie, pesé de tout leur poids dans la bataille de la dérégle- mentation: ouvrir les frontières du plus grand nombre de pays au 'libre flux de l'information' revenait à favoriser les mastodontes américains des industries de communication et des loisirs

(The United States, the main producer of new technology and the head- quarters of the main companies [in the field], has, in the interests of economic globalisation, thrown all of its weight into the battle for deregulation, with the opening-up of the frontiers of as many countries as possible to the 'free flow of information' being equivalent to favour- ing the US giants of the communications and leisure industries) (Ramonet, 1999: 179)

Globalisation, deregulation, new technology and the ideology of 'enter- tainment' are all perceived, rightly or wrongly, as instruments in a strategy for US domination.

On the cultural front, the literary critic Guy Scarpetta (1996: 29), criticises the transatlantic phenomenon known as 'political correctness' in the fol- lowing terms:

Il y a, aux États-Unis, la tyrannie du 'politically correct', qui fonctionne ouvertement comme une incitation à la censure et à l'autocensure, et qui vise à purifier la littérature de tout ce qui, en elle, pourrait donner une image 'non conforme' de certains groupes (femmes, minorités): véritable police de la représentation, dont on ne voit guère, si ses normes venaient à s'imposer, ce qui pourrait rester d'oeuvres comme celles de Faulkner, d'Hemingway ou de Philip Roth.

(In the United States, there is the tyranny of the 'politically correct', which functions quite openly as an incitement to censorship and self- censorship, with the aim of purifying literature of all elements which might give a 'non-approved' image of certain groups (women, minori- ties): a full-blooded policing of representation, whose rules, should they prevail, would surely leave almost nothing intact of the works of Faulkner, Hemingway or Philip Roth.)

On a similar note, this time in the field of psychoanalysis, the authors of a recent major work of reference, *Dictionnaire de la psychanalyse* (by Roudinesco & Plon, 1997: 166), denounce 'un double mouvement de "correction politique" et de conservatisme qui fit des ravages à cette époque dans la partie anglophone du continent américain' (a two-pronged movement of "political correctness" and conservatism that spread like wildfire in this period through English-speaking America'), concluding that these tendencies have, as things stand, 'mis en danger, aux États-Unis comme au Canada, l'existence même du freudisme, une fois encore violemment attaqué dans un contexte puritain' ('ended up threatening the very existence of Freudianism in the United States and Canada, such is the force of the present wave of attacks – not for the first time – in a context of puritanism').

From the language viewpoint, it may already be noted that the extracts quoted here themselves provide evidence for a certain terminological hesitation in French intellectual circles: where Scarpetta leaves the term 'politically correct' (used substantively) in English, Roudinesco and Plon, no doubt in order to demarcate themselves unambiguously from an ideology which they reject, *translate* it, as 'correction politique'. The hesitation over usage revealed by this divergence is – as we shall see later – in fact symptomatic of a general linguistic ambiguity that pervades contemporary French discourse. The question has to be asked: *Is it possible – or even desirable – to avoid the use of anglicisms when writing about the contemporary world in French?*

The French intellectual milieu of which these sources are representative is certainly not alone in its critical stance towards the USA. The charges made by the likes of Roudinesco and Plon, Scarpetta and Ramonet against that country's multinationals, its entertainment business and its neo-puritanism of both left and right find their echo in the commentaries of a number of transatlantic social critics. Thus, in the arena of globalisation, Noam Chomsky (1996) denounces the motives behind the US-led world trading system, as manifested in NAFTA or in the GATT/WTO set-up:

> American companies stand to gain $61 billion a year from the Third World if US protectionist demands are satisfied at GATT (as they are in NAFTA), at a cost to the South that will dwarf the current huge flow of debt-service capital from South to North. Such measures are designed to ensure that US-based corporations control the technology of the future, including biotechnology, which, it is hoped, will allow protected private enterprise to control health, agriculture and the means of life generally, locking the poor into dependence and hopelessness

In parallel, Benjamin R. Barber (1995: 89), attacks the tentacular global reach of Hollywood, in no uncertain terms:

> Movies and videos are ever more unitary in content as they become ever more global in distribution. More and more people around the world watch films that are less and less varied. Nowhere is American monoculture more evident or more feared than in its movies and videos.

Elsewhere in the cultural area, Harold Bloom, Professor of Humanities at Yale and possibly the best-known literary critic in the US today, in *The Western Canon: The Books and School of the Ages*, his polemical defence of traditional literature and learning (1994), repudiates both Christian fundamentalism *and* the 'politically correct' belief-system that dominates his country's campuses, affirming the need to 'combat the cultural politics, both Left and Right, that are destroying criticism and consequently may destroy literature itself' (p. 62), and darkly predicts that 'we are only a decade or less away from the dawning of a new Theocratic Age' (p. 148) – all in denunciatory tones that, if anything, exceed those of Scarpetta or Roudinesco and Plon.

If we now return across the Atlantic to France, it may now be interesting to examine the text of *Non merci, Oncle Sam!*, a book by Noël Mamère, a Green politician and former Member of the European Parliament, and Olivier Warin, a journalist (1999). This polemical volume brings together the various strands of anti-American critique, as manifested both inside and outside France – with Benjamin R. Barber cited as an authority – repeating the criticisms made in the examples quoted earlier (free-market evangelism, censorious neo-puritanism, mass-cultural domination) and making a number of further charges (obsessional use of the death penalty, rampant gun ownership, irresponsible promotion of GMOs, and even the export of Hallowe'en to France). The USA is accused, above all, of 'hégémonisme économique' ('economic hegemonism') and of promoting 'la dictature du marché' ('the dictatorship of the market') (p. 64, p. 18).

However, the authors' general argument, though carefully documented, suffers from a curious contradiction in the specific field of language. On the role of the English language in the world, the authors note in passing that 'la France . . . tente d'éradiquer les termes anglais de son vocabulaire' ('France . . . is trying to eradicate English terms from its vocabulary' – p. 180 – a point which will be taken up later in this article). They also – if, again, only briefly – repeat the view, often heard in certain French intellectual milieux, that the Internet is essentially a medium for US cultural (and therefore, presumably, linguistic) domination: 'nous allons tout droit "vers un nouveau siècle d'impérialisme américain", par le truchement de la maîtrise des réseaux électroniques mondiaux' ('we are heading straight "towards a new century of US imperialism", via the mastery of the worldwide electronic networks') – (p. 163); the authors here, like so many others in France, fail to understand that the Internet is by its nature qualitatively different from older media such as television, since it allows its consumers to be producers too, and any user is free not just to take material off the network but to put material on – *in any language*, not only English! These points apart, however, Mamère and Warin scarcely touch on the phenomenon – surely relevant to their main argument – of the US-led global reach of English.

The text of *Non merci, Oncle Sam*! is, nonetheless, liberally – and somewhat ironically, given its subject-matter – sprinkled with anglicisms. On the present writer's count, its 187 pages contain a total of 57 such words and phrases (excluding repetitions), which makes an average of almost one fresh anglicism every three pages. Some of these usages might be justifiable as tongue-in-cheek, while others could be explained by the specific nature of the subjects discussed. Nonetheless, this book contains a large number of anglicisms which seem quite simply unnecessary. These include: 'les téléspectateurs zappent' (p. 10), '[ils] surfent sur le Web' (p. 17), 'le *lobby* agroalimentaire' (p. 42), 'de confortables portefeuilles de stock-options' (p. 49), 'les gangs russes' (p. 89), 'un véritable "boom" de l'industrie privée de l'emprisonnement' (p. 137), 'le record du monde des serial-killers' (p. 165), 'la publicité ou [le] marketing' (p. 185). There is no *a priori* reason why all these anglicisms – even where italicised or put in quotation marks – could not have been replaced by genuine French words or phrases: 'sautent d'une chaîne à l'autre' for 'zappent', 'naviguent sur la Toile' for 'surfent sur le Web', 'les groupes de pression' for 'le *lobby*', 'droits de souscription' for 'stock-options', 'bandes de truands' for 'gangs', 'essor' for 'boom', 'plus grand nombre' for 'record', 'tueurs en série' for 'serial-killers', 'mercatique' for 'marketing'. Arguably, the presence of these anglicisms can only be understood as a manifestation, on an unconscious or semi-conscious level, of *precisely that submission to US mass-cultural hegemony* which, on a conscious level, the two authors reject, and *opposition to which* is actually the raison d'être of their book!

### Anglicisms and Their Vicissitues – Linguistic and Sociolinguistic Aspects

Having established, through these telling examples, something of the persistence and extent of anglicisms in French, we may now take a closer look at the characteristics of the phenomenon from a linguistic point of view. Words originating in English can pass through a whole series of vicissitudes in French, generating 'new' forms which no native speaker of English would recognise as genuine. The possible transformations are legion, and pseudo-English forms have come into being across the whole range of linguistic levels.

On the lexical level, modern French usage includes pseudo-anglicisms in the form of words that are non-existent in English: these may be invented nouns, such as 'le rugbyman', 'le tennisman', 'le recordman' (for 'rugby player', '(male) tennis player' and '(male) record holder'), or verbal nouns which scarcely exist in English as separate lexical items, such as 'le lifting' (for 'facelift') or 'le forcing' (approximately, an 'extra push'). On the semantic level, an English word may acquire a new meaning in French: 'le spot' has come to designate what is known in Britain as a commercial. Indeed, lexical items can undergo both a semantic and a morphological shift, as in the curious case of 'le pin's' (in English, 'badge'), where 'pin' has acquired the meaning of 'badge' by association, and, not content with that, has changed case to the genitive! A legitimate English noun such as 'le snob' may generate a 'new' French verb: 'snober' has established itself as an alternative to the native 'bouder', although no verb 'to snob' exists in English. Alternatively, the '-er' suffix may serve to naturalise an actually existing English verb, as in 'shooter' ('to shoot' in the cinematic sense) or the dubious IT dyad 'uploader'/'downloader'; another naturalisation strategy is to invent a French abbreviation for an English word, as in 'le pull' for 'pullover', or, dare one add, 'McDo' for the much-disliked yet much-patronised McDonald's. An English term may also be semi-assimilated by gallicising the spelling, as in 'le bogue' ('computer bug'), a form which alternates in current usage with the more visibly alien 'le bug'. For nouns, assimilation also requires the assignation of a gender; and, if the obvious temptation is to give semantically neutral anglicisms masculine status (e.g. 'le fax'), the goal of naturalisation has, in some cases, been better served by the choice of the feminine gender, as in the use – for a media personality of either sex – of 'la star' (probably by analogy with the two grammatically feminine but semantically sex-neutral native terms, 'la vedette' and 'l'étoile').

Pseudo-anglicisms are, then, a quite widespread phenomenon in today's French, in line with a long-established tendency (after all, no native speaker of English would accept 'shampooing' as a synonym for 'shampoo' or 'self' on its own as meaning 'self-service restaurant'). The 'pseudo' nature of such forms may well not be recognised by native French speakers, who are likely to assume they are genuine English forms, and to be surprised if, say, a real live anglophone fails to understand 'le baby-foot' ('bar football'). Indeed, even the experts may slip up: the *Dictionnaire des Difficultés du Français* (Robert, 1994), includes in its entry 'Anglais (mots)' a reference to 'le recordman' (recommended plural: 'les recordmen') which fails to specify that this term is actually not an English word at all – although, conversely, the *Petit Larousse illustré* for 2000 (Larousse, 1999; hereinafter '*Larousse 2000*') redeems Gallic lexicographical honour by correctly designating the same word as a 'faux anglicisme'.

At all events, there is no doubt that contemporary French writing in the journalistic register (newspapers, magazines, topical non-fiction books) is strewn with words and phrases deriving from English, whether they are genuine British and/or American forms or pseudo-anglicisms (as much is clear from our previous analysis above of Mamère and Warin's book). The phenomenon affects most areas of topical or public discourse (with the major exceptions of domestic politics and, above all, the law, where the difference of legal systems acts as an effective barrier to anglicisms of any provenance).

It may now be interesting to consider briefly, from a sociolinguistic perspective, some of the possible motives for so widespread an employment of alien terms by writers and journalists, in what is, after all, a country that remains particularly conscious of its specific cultural identity. Among the factors that may be identified are the following:

(1) *Terminological rigour*: an equivalent French word or phrase for the concept may not exist (or may exist only as a long-winded paraphrase). Where a French journalist is writing on a culturally or institutionally specific subject in an English-speaking country, he or she is obviously best advised not to translate terms which may have no exact equivalent. However, certain general subject areas, including some marked by a substantial Anglo-American conceptual input, have evolved their own terminology in French. This is particularly true of the computer/ Internet field, which we shall look at in some detail later. However, even here there are terms for which no French equivalent exists; for instance, no-one has yet come up with a true Gallic translation of 'spam', the jargon term for electronic junk mail (despite, or because of, that term's origin in the nether reaches of British cuisine) and, for the moment 'le spam', 'le spammeur' and 'spammer' rule, even if none of them figures in *Larousse 2000*!

(2) *Sectoral jargon*: in some subject areas, there is a whole arsenal of ready-made English-language terminology that is also highly specific. An example here is the world of non-classical musics, which has not evolved its own French terminology in the same way as the computer world has. Native French terms, such as 'la chanson' and 'les variétés', do of course exist, but in the case of specific genres the tendency has long been simply to import the English term. This phenomenon goes back to the early 20th century, with 'le ragtime', 'le jazz' and 'le blues', and has in recent years has been responsible for such usages as 'le rap', 'la techno', 'le trip-hop', etc. A curious case is provided by 'la world' (for 'world music'), which might have seemed an unnecessary import since a native term, 'les musiques du monde', already existed; by now, however, in practice the French term has come to be reserved for 'genuine' ethnic music of the field-recording type, whereas 'la world' usually denotes 'contemporary' ethnic music produced using modern

studio techniques, or else music resulting from fusions between different ethnic genres or between such genres and mainstream Anglo-
American popular forms.

(3) *Brevity*: 'le flop' is shorter than 'l'échec', 'le boom' than 'l'essor', 'la star'
than 'la vedette'. This is, of course, a practical consideration in certain
contexts, e.g. newspaper headlines.

(4) *Comprehensibility*: the 'approved' French word may not be readily
understood. 'Le fax/faxer' are likely to be understood where 'la
télécopie/le télécopieur/envoyer par télécopie' are not; the same
applies to 'scanner/le scanneur' as against 'numériser/le numériseur'.

(5) *Unconscious pro-American reflexes*, as an expression of fashion or as a
result of over-exposure to US media. Such reflexes may account for,
say, the widespread contemporary use of 'le kidnapping/kidnapper/
le kidnappeur', instead of the older 'enlèvement/enlever/ravisseur'.
Another factor here may be the naturalisation of transatlantic free-
market values and the attendant mass-consumption lifestyle – hence
'le management' for 'la gestion', 'le chewing-gum' for 'la gomme à
mâcher', etc.

(6) (conversely) *An ironic anti-Americanism*, which may dictate a conscious
use of the English word, as a strategy to distance the French writer (and
reader) from the US values being attacked. Possible examples here are
'le business/le businessman' (with specifically American connotations, as opposed to the more general 'les affaires/l'homme
d'affaires'), and 'le serial-killer' (for 'le tueur en série'), in contexts
where certain US phenomena (the free-market system, endemic social
violence) are being openly called in question.

The French writer is also free to choose *not* to use anglicisms, and the
deliberate selection of a French lexical item may be motivated by various
factors, among them:

(1) *Officially organised hostility to anglicisms*. The existence of this tendency
in France and the French-speaking world generally, and the consequent attempts to reduce the incidence of the phenomenon, are well
known enough. The special case of Quebec, the francophone territory
which lies geographically closest to the USA, unfortunately falls
outside the scope of the present study; the usual view, however, is that
Québécois French has succeeded better than any other variant of the
language in keeping anglicisms down and out. In France, it is the
official business of the 'Académie française' (the French Academy) to
devise French equivalents to English neologisms. This activity is typically derided by the British, as representing the *dirigiste* antithesis to
Britain's own empiricist traditions; as the grammarian Professor John

Honey (1997) puts it in his book *Language Is Power: The Story of Standard English and its Enemies*, 'Britain has always resisted the idea of language management by an official body, especially an Academy' (p. 144). Nonetheless, the French Academy's coinages have in some notable instances succeeded in imposing themselves, especially in the computer field: 'l'informatique' ('computer science'), 'l'ordinateur' ('computer'), 'le matériel' ('hardware') and 'le logiciel' ('software') have all become standard usage in France. Other officially approved concoctions ('le palmarès' for 'hit-parade', 'la mercatique' for 'marketing') have been markedly less successful, although *Larousse 2000* dutifully lists such forms alongside the prevalent anglicism, with the remark 'recommandation officielle' ('official recommendation').

(2) *The spontaneous generation of genuine French equivalents.* It occasionally happens that a genuine French counterpart to a US term springs up from the grassroots. A notable recent example, in the context of the WTO and the related controversies, is 'la malbouffe' for 'junk food' (a case of linguistic 'bovéisme'?). Another case in point is the currently fashionable phrase 'dans tous ses états' (literally 'in all his/her/its states'; 'viewed from every side', also 'nervous, agitated'), as in 'Le bogue dans tous ses états', the headline given by *Le Monde* to its report of 22 December 1999 on the millennium bug. This is an interesting case of re-assimilation, since the present vogue for this phrase actually derives from the French title of a recent American film, Woody Allen's *Deconstructing Harry*: the translator, instead of resorting to 'déconstruction' – even though that is a true French intellectual term, deriving from the work of the eminently Gallic philosopher Jacques Derrida – came up with a totally different title, *Harry dans tous ses états*, thus giving a whole new lease of life to a native French phrase.

(3) *Conscious and systematic 'localisation' within a sector of activity*, leading to the creation of an entire terminological artillery in French. This has, to a large extent, happened in the computer/Internet field, where, for obvious operational reasons, a term has to have a specific and non-negotiable meaning. By now, a comprehensive arsenal of French computer terms exists – far more so than in other Romance languages. In the case of the basic terms 'ordinateur' ('computer') and 'logiciel' ('software'), French may be contrasted with Spanish, where 'el ordenador' has established itself (at least in Spain) but 'el software' is the norm, and, even more so, with Portuguese, which has not managed to improve on 'o computador', and Italian, in which, although 'l'elaboratore' and the no longer very accurate 'il calcolatore' are possible synonyms, in practice 'il computer' is the norm. The entire lexicon of the world's most commonly-used operating system has been

laboriously translated into French, and it is those terms, not the English ones, that appear on the Gallic user's screen ('gestionnaire de fichiers' for 'file manager', 'panneau de configuration' for 'control panel', etc.). Even so, not all French IT coinages have succeeded: 'le shareware' and 'le freeware' are far more likely to be found than 'le partagiciel' and 'le graticiel'; and the coinages 'le fureteur' and 'le butineur' have made little headway against 'le browser'. In some cases, current usage hesitates between the French term and the anglicism, as in 'le fichier attaché' or 'l'attachment', 'le lien' or 'le link', 'la Toile' or 'le Web'. In the last-named case, French adds an alternative sense deriving from a compression that does not operate in English, for by now-established usage 'le Web' can mean either 'the World Wide Web' or (e.g. in advertisements) 'an individual website'. Conversely, however, where a genuine French term is employed, there are cases where French has evolved greater sophistication than English in differentiating senses: for 'email' (assuming the English word is not used), French has evolved 'la messagerie' or 'le courrier électronique' for the function, and 'le courriel / le mél', as two alternative forms for an individual message (or for an email address). In addition, the French translations of '(Net)surf' and '(Net)surfer', 'naviguer' and 'le cybernaute / l'internaute', may be considered rather more intelligent than the English originals, since their navigation and sailing images imply a purposive search, whereas 'surf', with its connotations of arbitrariness and superficiality, is actually based on a false analogy with 'channel-surfing', coming from a quite different medium, namely television. In practice, nonetheless, 'surfer' and 'le Netsurfeur' remain more common than their ingeniously concocted French equivalents.

At this point, we may return to the detailed examination of anglicisms in particular texts. For this purpose, we shall now look at three recent articles from a single issue of a representative publication, namely the 10–22 December 1999 issue of the magazine *Le Nouvel Économiste*, covering two of the subject-areas which have already come up for examination in this article, namely world trade and the computer / Internet field.

The issue concerned contains, in the wake of the 1999 WTO interministerial conference in Seattle, two articles on world trade: an editorial, 'Les leçons de Seattle' ('The lessons of Seattle'), by Jean-Michel Quatrepoint (p. 3); and a news feature, 'Comment surmonter les divergences de Seattle' ('How to move beyond the disagreements of Seattle'), by Philippe Plassart (pp. 32–5). The editorial pulls off the tour de force of discussing globalised trade while perpetrating only one solitary anglicism. Jean-Michel Quatrepoint attacks US isolationism, declaring: 'L'échec de la conférence de l'OMC n'est pas tant celui de la mondialisation que celui d'une certaine Amérique' ('The failure of the WTO summit is not so much that of globalisation as that of a certain America'). He concludes: 'Et s'il est un slogan qui devrait survivre à Seattle, c'est bien que "le monde n'est pas un simple marchandise"' ('And if there's a slogan which deserves to survive Seattle, it's "the world is not just a commodity"'), rather unfortunately marring his closing flourish with the article's sole anglicism, 'slogan' (rather than 'devise'; to be fair, this is actually a word of Scottish Gaelic origin, but it is unlikely the author is aware of that). This lapse apart, across the article the editorialist skilfully manages to avoid the traps set by his subject-matter: he employs 'conférence', not 'summit', 'société informationnelle', not 'information society', 'libre-échange', not 'free trade'. By contrast, however, the longer news feature on the WTO includes – despite the broadly critical slant of its content – no less than 15 anglicisms, many of them avoidable. Its author, Philippe Plassart, opens his post mortem with the laconic comment: 'Flop' – rather than 'échec' or even the Italian-derived 'fiasco', though both words do, to be fair, crop up later in his text. Other anglicisms in his text include 'les rounds de l'OMC' (despite the existence of 'cycle' as an alternative to 'round'), 'le business yankee' (this may of course be ironic), 'cet ex-hippie militant' (the French 'soixante-huitard' – '68-er' – would provide at least an approximate equivalent), 'l'e-business américain' (why not 'commerce électronique'?), 'le dramatique crash du Boeing d'Egyptair' ('catastrophe' would convey the meaning of 'crash' quite sufficiently). The journalist's reading of the summit carefully avoids identification with any of the parties, and is far from sycophantic to either the US administration or the American NGOs, suggesting, indeed, as regards the latter, that 'la tour de Babel de la contestation anti-OMC n'en finissait pas d'aligner les contradictions de la société américaine' ('the Tower of Babel of the anti-WTO protests cease-lessly pointed up the contradictions of US society'). At the same time, nonetheless, his text, *considered in its linguistic dimension*, leaves an ambivalent aftertaste similar to that paradoxically produced by Mamère and Warin's anti-American tract.

    If we now move to the subject of the Internet, we find, in the same issue, an article by Jean-Jerôme Bertolus and Marie-Anne Garigue, entitled 'La France bascule dans l'Internet' ('France moves on to the Internet'; 10–22 December 1999, pp. 24–30) – which exhibits, not unsurprisingly, no less than 25 anglicisms. While the core terminology used displays a certain oscillation ('Internet' alternates with 'le Réseau', 'le Web' with 'la Toile') and certain specifically French terms such as 'internaute' do get a look-in, in many instances the authors quite visibly take the line of least resistance and borrow the English term nearest to hand. Thus, we find in their text: 'Ils sont des centaines de milliers ... à échanger des e-mails, ... à rechercher un job sur les sites d'emploi' ('In their hundreds of thousands . . . they exchange emails . . . and look for jobs on situations-vacant sites'); 'ils veulent juste des snacks ouverts 24 heures sur 24' ('they just want snack-bars open 24 hours a day'); 'ce manager a créé Arbizon Multimédia' ('This manager set up Arbizon Multimédia'); 'tee-shirt, haut débit et fun' ('T-shirt, high performance and fun'); 'le directeur du marketing' ('the market-ing director'); 'cette start-up star de la Bourse' ('this start-up star of the Stock Exchange'); 'leur business plan' ('their business plan'), etc. These examples reveal two more than arguably dangerous tendencies, both relating to the uncritical replication of transatlantic attitudes which are in reality highly ideological. One is the wholesale assimilation of American free-market values, as reflected in the use of 'business plan', 'manager, 'marketing', 'job', 'start-up star', etc. The other, equally insidious, is what might be called 'Disneyfication', the naturalisation of the 'entertainment' values of US mass culture, as manifested in usages like 'fun' (why not the native 'divertissement'?), 'snack' (for 'snack-bar'; as if France did not have its 'brasseries', or Belgium its 'friteries'!), and, indeed, 'tee-shirt' (this spelling, all too common in France, is, to compound matters, a solecism creating a false etymology – as if the English word were a golfing term, when in fact it derives from the letter-T shape of the garment!). While there is no doubt that greater French use of the Internet will increase the sum total of French-language texts available on the network, lexical attitudes such as those shown by the authors of this article give reason to fear that the French sent out into cyberspace may often leave much to desire in authenticity.

## Anglicicms in Context

From the examples we have looked at, the conclusion is inevitable that in numerous circumstances – especially in contexts directly relating to globalisation in its various aspects – contemporary French writing in the journalistic register is, as a matter of habit, liberally sprinkled with angli-cisms, the vast majority of which originate in the USA. At this point, some – such as those pundits who reject the notion of 'dumbing-down' and applaud the alleged worldwide benefits of transatlantic mass culture – might argue that there is nothing to worry about in this phenomenon, be it for French or for any other language. Linguistic miscegenation, it could be argued, might actually prove a cultural and communicational asset, improving writers' expressiveness by allowing them to draw on the resources of different cultures.

This is a potentially interesting point – English itself was, after all, origi-nally the product of a miscegenation between Anglo-Saxon and Latin/

French elements – but a serious problem arises over defending anglicisms in French on such grounds, namely the question of (in)equality. The situation as between France and the US may be illuminated by comparison with the state of affairs in India. In that country, two languages, English and Hindi, have *de facto* lingua franca status, while a total of 17 languages have official status at regional level, and the number of languages and dialects actually spoken is estimated in hundreds. English and Hindi, in particular, have cross-fertilised each other over time. Hindi has absorbed such terms as 'bank' and 'train', while any newspaper article in Indian English will feature, embedded into syntactically perfect English, such assimilated terms as 'lakh' (100,000), 'crore' (10 million), 'dacoit' (armed robber), 'chawl' (apartment block), etc. Half a century after independence, the continued use of English by now has little to do with colonialism and much to do with practicality: independent India has had relatively little institutional contact with Britain and even less with the USA, but English is the only language used in the subcontinent in which educated speakers and writers from all language groups can understand each other (in the southern states, where the autochthonous languages are not Indo-European but Dravidian, Hindi is quite as 'alien' as English). Salman Rushdie wrote in 1983:

> The children of independent India seem not to think of English as being irredeemably tainted by its colonial provenance. They use it as an Indian language, as one of the tools they have to hand . . . In South India . . . the resentment of Hindi is far greater than of English . . . English is an essential language in India, not only because of its technical vocabularies and the international communication which it makes possible, but also simply to permit two Indians to talk together in a tongue which neither party hates' ('"Commonwealth literature" does not exist'). (see Rushdie, 1991: 65–6)

In these circumstances, with Indian English established as a home-grown language variant, it is quite possible for English and Hindi to compete on equal terms, and therefore to influence each other on a reciprocal basis.

By contrast, the problem with anglicisms (for which, read americanisms) in contemporary French is that the relationship is *not* reciprocal. One has only to ask a simple question to make this clear: *how many French words are being naturalised today in American English?* The relationship between French and US English is not an equal one: it is predicated on the economic, military and mass-cultural power of the USA. Those concerned about the survival of the unique expressive character of French (or any other language) may wish to conclude that the use of anglicisms in French (and all other languages) should be confined to the absolute minimum (to phenomena specific to anglophone countries, and to technical terms where a reasonably concise local equivalent has not emerged) and that all writing professionals could arguably make a constant and conscious effort to use anglicisms as little as possible.

## The Situation in the European Parliament

Following this picture of the relationship between English and French as it exists in the world at large, I shall now consider the rather different question of the interaction between the two languages, from the viewpoint of anglicisms in French, as it displays itself in the work of a particular international institution, namely the European Parliament.

The European Union (or European Communities) and its institutions are committed in principle to multilingualism and language equality: the EU is the only international organisation which makes laws which are binding on its Member States and which have to be incorporated in every detail into domestic legislation – a provision which makes translation into every national language absolutely imperative. The EU currently has 11 working languages and 12 official languages (the 12th being Irish, into which the Treaties and certain basic legislation are translated, while for ordinary legislation Ireland accepts the English texts). Nonetheless, where the EU's day-to-day business is concerned the language regime used in practice varies from one institution to another. The European Commission produces the majority of its original documents in English or French; it thus translates all documents *into* every working language, but relatively few *out of* languages other than French and English.

The European Parliament, which prides itself on being the Union's sole directly elected body, has thus far operated a regime of full multilingualism for its official documents: legislative texts may be written in any of the 11 working languages, and must be translated into all of them. This ensures that MEPs can debate and vote on texts which they have read in their native language, thus avoiding any kind of *de facto* language inequality between MEPs from different Member States. Nonetheless, for the Parliament's day-to-day *internal* business, a simplified practical regime prevails: internal communication, oral or written, effectively takes place in the two languages that play a lingua franca role within the institution, namely English and French.

At the beginning, French was the Parliament's (and the Communities') sole lingua franca, but after Britain's and Ireland's accession in 1973 it was joined by English. English is today an official language in two Member States, and French in three (France, Belgium and Luxembourg). English is usually favoured as a lingua franca within the Parliament by citizens of the northern Member States (those from Germany, Austria, the Netherlands and the three Nordic Member States, as well as Flemish speakers from Belgium), and French by the southerners (those from Italy, Spain, Portugal and Greece). The balance has shifted somewhat in favour of English since the most recent wave of accessions (Austria, Sweden and Finland), but this has not fundamentally shaken the entrenched status of French. Thus, such documents as staff notices, messages from the administration, trade union tracts, etc., are generally distributed, whether by paper or electronic channels, in English and French.

The two languages with lingua franca status have, not surprisingly, engaged over the years in a certain degree of miscegenation (the examples which follow belong either to the parlance of the EU institutions in general or to the specific argot of the Parliament, or to both). English as used within the EU has accepted such gallicisms as 'the acquis communautaire' (the existing body of Community legislation) and 'stage/stagiaire' (trainee-ship/trainee). In day-to-day administrative practice, English-speaking officials of Parliament use French terms like 'feuille de route' (transmission sheet) and 'responsable' (the official responsible for a document). Some native anglophones, both within and outside the institutions, might complain at what they would no doubt perceive as linguistic contamination, but it remains the fact that the British chose not to join the European Communities at the beginning, preferring to remain aloof. Hugo Young (1998), in his recent historical study of the 'Britain-in-Europe' question, quotes a senior civil servant at Britain's Foreign Office, at the time of the 1955 Messina Conference which set up the European Coal and Steel Community (ECSC), the forbear of today's EU, as writing: 'There can of course be no question of our entering any organisation of a supranational capacity' (p. 82). Britain did not join the ECSC at the moment of its founding, nor did it join the European Economic Community on its inception in 1957. Had the British become members from the outset, rather than 16 years after the EC's foundation, they would have had the chance to influence the institutions' administrative culture and, therefore, the nature of the language used in them, from year zero. As it was, France was the only one of the victorious post-war powers to be a founder member, and had the inbuilt advantage of French being an official language in 50% of the original Member States – which were, besides, being also the three chosen to host the Communities' institutions, in Brussels, Luxembourg and Strasbourg. The nation of Voltaire was therefore self-evidently in a position to create an instant administrative and linguistic hegemony.

Today, however, the balance is not what it was, and the French used within the Parliament is increasingly spattered with anglicisms. The French texts concerned are very often produced by officials *who are not native speakers of either English or French*, but the same anglicisms may be observed in material written by French or francophone-Belgian native speakers. This phenomenon is particularly acute in the computer field. Internal documents written in French relating to the Parliament's IT systems very often contain such dubious hybrids as 'uploader/downloader' (for 'charger/télécharger'), 'le password' (for 'mot de passe'), 'updater' (for 'mettre à jour'). In one of the most bizarre cases, the English 'directory' (in the computer sense), habitually rendered not by the correct French translation 'le répertoire' but by 'le directory', has even spawned, in occasional Parliament usage, the anomalous term 'le directoire' – perhaps in homage to the post-revolutionary government organ of that name set up in the France of 1795 . . .

The use of hybrid language of this nature leads to a number of communication problems, of which English native speakers may in practice be more aware than most. For a native anglophone, it can be extremely problematic to have to deal with a French text liberally and unpredictably spattered with anglicisms, pseudo-anglicisms or bizarre derivatives like 'le directoire'. If an anglophone replies in French to a message, itself in French, from a Spanish or Greek colleague, should that anglophone answer using a genuine French term like 'télécharger' or stick, in order to be understood, to the non-authentic 'downloader'? This difficulty becomes particularly acute when transposed to the oral register: how should the English native speaker pronounce 'le login' when on the telephone to a francophone colleague (as in English or as in French?), and if 'charger' is not understood at a meeting of IT personnel of multiple national origins, how ought the dreaded 'uploader' to be pronounced? This kind of acrobatic macaronics, with all its complications, could be avoided if computer matters were discussed in either genuine English or genuine French: since the French terms exist, there is no defensible reason for not using them.

## Conclusions

If, on the various grounds suggested here, there is good reason for considering the phenomenon of anglicisms in today's French to be a largely negative development, then it would be useful for international organisations committed to a multicultural philosophy – the European Parliament being one such body – to develop a proactive policy to discourage the use of such anglicisms, in French and in all the other languages used. An international body's in-house training services should, for example, be perfectly capable of devising and offering courses in, for example, computer English *and* computer French. What is needed is more linguistic awareness in general, specific awareness of this particular insidious problem, and the political will to remedy it.

Meanwhile, in the world in general, it is well enough known that France is the Member State spearheading the EU's position at the WTO in favour of preserving 'cultural diversity'. This policy applies in the first place to the audiovisual sector, but cultural diversity obviously implies linguistic diversity. The price of linguistic diversity is, however, eternal vigilance; and those who preach diversity in international forums could usefully remember that vigilance begins at home.

## References
Barber, Benjamin R. (1995) *Jihad vs. McWorld: How Globalism and Tribalism are Reshaping the World*. New York: Ballantine.

Bloom, Harold (1994) *The Western Canon: The Books and School of the Ages*. London: Macmillan.

Chomsky, Noam (1996) Notes on NAFTA: The masters of mankind. http://www.cs.unb.ca/~alopez-o/politics/chomnafta.html.

*Dictionnaire des Difficultés du Français* (1994). Paris: Robert.

Honey, John (1997) *Language Is Power: The Story of Standard English and its Enemies*. London: Faber and Faber.

*Le Monde* (1999) Informatique [Supplement], 22 December, p. vi.

Mamère, Noël and Warin, Olivier (1999) *Non merci, Oncle Sam!* Paris: Ramsay.

*Petit Larousse illustré 2000*. Paris: Larousse.

Ramonet, Ignacio (1999) *La tyrannie de la communication*. Paris: Éditions Galilée.

Roudinesco, Elisabeth and Plon, Michel (1997) *Dictionnaire de la psychanalyse*. Paris: Fayard.

Rushdie, Salman (1991) 'Commonwealth literature' does not exist. In *Imaginary Homelands*. London: Granta (originally published in 1983).

Scarpetta, Guy (1996) 'La littérature en procès'. *La Règle du Jeu*, No. 18, January 1996, pp. 28–36.

Young, Hugo (1998) *This Blessed Plot: Britain and Europe from Churchill to Blair*. London: Macmillan.

## Chapter 4

# *Translation of EU Legal Texts*

RENATO CORREIA

Towards the end of the 1930s a great name in the history of European ideas wrote an illuminating piece on translation which I should like to take as the starting point. Forced by his country's civil war into exile in South America, where he continued to work in defence of the humanism whose mantle he had inherited, the Spanish philosopher José Ortega y Gasset (1970) published an essay in the guise of an imaginary debate, and this essay has since become a familiar landmark for all those interested in translation: 'Miseria y Esplendor de la Traducción'. Drawing on the tradition of the *Sprachphilosophie* of Wilhelm von Humboldt with which he is well acquainted, Ortega y Gasset points out that there is not a one-to-one relationship between languages, between the cultures to which they belong or even between the geographical areas in which they have developed. This means, for instance, that what a Spaniard calls *bosque* is not quite the same as what a German refers to as *Wald:* not only is the vegetation rather dissimilar, but also – more importantly – the mental and emotional associations are almost completely different. Any translation thus remains 'an impossible venture' ('*un propósito imposible*'). And yet, paradoxically, that very impossibility is what encourages us to translate. In so doing we realise with some dismay that however hard we marshal our resources and draw on our experience, the end result will never be the same as the text with which we started. Hence there is a utopian element in treating the labour of translation as the pursuit of textual identity, although it is true that for Ortega y Gasset, the utopian element is present in most human endeavours worthy of the name.

To these two ideas – the paradox and utopia of translation – I should like to propose adding a third, namely the cultural *convention* which, in spite of all the evidence, expects the source text and the target text to coincide. This means that the translator and those who request or use translations pretend that the translated text is the same as the starting text, apart from the language, whereas it is seldom possible to change the language without changing some other elements. That is, the text is changed. What is undeniably at work here is a *fiction,* not in the ordinary pejorative sense of the word, but in the positive, approving sense supplied by economists and lawyers. They define it as a process for postulating a fact or situation that differs from reality in order to derive some practical benefit. If in our case the benefit makes it possible for people who speak different languages to communicate with one another, we can only welcome the fiction and do our best to perpetuate it.

## The Paradoxical Nature of Translation

One may wonder of what use these ideas may be for translators on the verge of the third millennium, with access to high-tech software, extensive online databases, computer-assisted translation programs and even, in some cases, automated translation. Where is the paradox, utopia or fiction in the work they do? What is the point of reviving a rather dusty axiom on the theoretical impossibility of translation and on its paradoxical character in practice?

I shall try briefly to explain why I think that the subject is still relevant and that the issues it raises should be seen in a new light. I am persuaded that translators in the Community institutions are more exposed than most to the old paradox of translation. To support this claim some reference must be made to the multilingual nature of Community law and the role of translation in this area, bearing in mind that the European Communities are primarily communities based on law. Moreover, with the adoption of the Treaty of Amsterdam, Parliament's role as co-legislator will grow substantially and its translators will thus increasingly be expected to work on legislative texts. Consequently there are good theoretical and practical reasons for giving the subject serious thought.

The main question appears reasonably straightforward. Is it possible to compile the same legislative provisions in the different languages? This is what the Community legal system requires, since the principle of legal universality implies that all European citizens must be governed by the *same* laws. To answer the question, we can postulate the principle that the different language versions will be identical, on condition that we omit the fact that translation intervenes during the legislative process. This postulation is necessary simply because the very concept of multilingual law is incompatible with the idea of translation.

This notion requires clarification. In April 1958, shortly after the treaties of Rome took effect, the Community legislator (the Council) adopted the first two regulations of all secondary law, determining the languages to be used by the two European Communities that had been founded: Regulation No. 1 EEC and Regulation No. 1 EAEC, the content of both being identical.[1] These Acts established the Community's multilingual system, and have not been amended in the 40 years that have elapsed since, apart from the addition of other official and working languages. Modifications have hence been quantitative not qualitative.

The wording of Article 4 of these regulations, which is still the legal basis for translation activities in the EU, is as follows: 'Les règlements et les autres textes de portée générale sont rédigés dans les quatre langues officielles [Regulations and other documents of general application shall be drafted in the four (now 11) official languages]'. To draw attention to the significance of this wording, I should like also to consider the verb corresponding to the French participle *rédigés* in the other three official languages at that time – namely Dutch, German and Italian: *gesteld*, *abgefaßt* and *redatti*. How should the legislator's use of this verb be interpreted? In practice, translators know all too well that parallel and simultaneous drafting in all the languages very rarely happens, but that a single language version, of one kind or another, is alway the starting point for the production of the others by the act of translation, which is thus behind ten of the 11 language versions eventually adopted. In legal terms, however, translation is inconceivable as a stage in the legislative procedure; to admit, by making explicit provision for the fact, that translators take part in the drafting of multilingual laws would mean sharing with them the power of law-making and this is the exclusive province of the legislator.

The topic raises enormous implications which I shall not deal with in further detail here, however. I shall move on to the Community's special legal and linguistic environment where translators are facing a new form of the paradox mentioned earlier. In practice, Community law is inconceivable *without* translation, whereas in strictly legal terms Community law is inconceivable *with it.*

One could say that translation is implicitly assimilated to the act of legislative drafting in several languages. To enable the legislator to 'draft' single-handedly in all the official languages the translator must not be perceived. Only the paradoxical fact that translation is substantially present in the Community legislative process, although officially absent from the legislation itself, makes it possible to safeguard the unique nature of EU law in all its linguistic plurality and diversity. EU translators are aware of the decisive part they have always played, without leaving the shadows themselves, to enable others to overcome the barriers of language and culture by way of the translators' skills as writers.

In the field of Community law translators must remain in the shadows in the search for equivalent solutions in the different languages. 'Equivalence in difference' was the byword used in the 1950s by an eminent representative of modern linguistics, Roman Jakobson, to define translation. The idea of 'equivalence' has been discredited in recent decades, where it concerns the theory of translation and linguistics in general, especially after it was shown, in a singular case of infinite regression, that the English and German forms of the term – *equivalence* and *Äquivalenz* – were not themselves equivalent (Snell-Hornby, 1988). Where Community law is concerned, however, the term 'equivalence' not only remains valid but also has a rare chance to deploy its full semantic content. As is well known, the various language versions of the regulations and other European 'laws' are 'equivalent' in the strict sense of the word, since they have the same legal value and can be invoked indiscriminately, in appeals to the Court of Justice for instance, by EU citizens or businesses, irrespective of their Member State of origin or that country's official language or languages. And yet translators well know that for linguistic and cultural reasons this equivalence can never be absolute. It can only be an approximation because – again paradoxically – there are different degrees of equivalence. It is the translator's job to find the best linguistic equivalences, in order to safeguard the legal equivalence of multilingual law as far as possible.[2]

## Translating Means Choosing

This is then the central issue that translation raises in the legislative field. Let us now see whether the same is true in the realm of politics, bearing in mind that the distinction between the two sectors is an artificial one since they overlap and interlock to some degree.

It is necessary to recall that translation is always a decision-making process. As a general rule, the problems posed by translating a text do not necessarily have only one solution; so the act of translating has something in common with political activity, since the two fields pre-eminently share a need to take decisions. The decisions are, of course, primarily linguistic ones, but when the text for translation contains a political message or will serve as the basis for political decisions, there will be an obvious political impact. 'Traduire, c'est choisir' – translating means choosing, to quote the title of an article published by Pierre-François Caillé in 1967, in the journal *Babel*. Translating means choosing and, ideally, choosing well. A good choice involves not only selecting the most appropriate linguistic resources; it also means, and this is a fundamental requirement in political texts, distinguishing between elements that need formulating clearly and others that will have to be rendered rather imprecisely, or even remain unexpressed.

In this regard I should like to mention a document I translated which deals with the drafting quality of Community legislation, in connection

with the European Commission's annual report entitled 'Better Lawmaking'.[3] Here is what the draftsman for the Committee on Institutional
Affairs[4] says on the subject: a real improvement in the clarity and comprehensibility of texts may run aground on two unavoidable problems, one of
which derives from the fact that 'decision-making at European level often
involves complex compromises that entail some degree of linguistic obscurity' (or as the first, German, version of the draft opinion puts it, 'eine
sprachliche Unschärfe' [some linguistic unfocused-ness]).

   This is an accurate description of the main difficulty faced by translators:
if they lack sufficient information on the preceding debate and the compromise that was reached in it, how is this linguistic obscurity to be correctly
interpreted, and how should it be re-created in the other versions? How are
translators to distinguish the deliberate obscurity that is the expression of a
political and often hard-won compromise from another kind of obscurity –
the inadvertent kind produced when those drafting the original version
use a language that is not their mother tongue?

   Translating means choosing; but how does one make the right choice
when the best linguistic solutions might be undesirable, because they could
have unintended political or legislative consequences? How, on the other
hand, does one discover what specific linguistic solutions should be chosen
when they are required for legislative or political reasons in certain documents? In situations like this, which are likely to become more frequent in
future, explicit guidelines or detailed instructions need to be provided.

   I realise I am touching here on an aspect that may offend the sensibilities
of many colleagues, who might well take an unfavourable view of any
attempt to question the translator's freedom of choice. Some discussion
will certainly be needed to prevent any misunderstandings in this area,
while avoiding the hazards of a philosophical debate on freedom of action
in general, which would go far beyond questions of translation. I shall limit
myself to two points. First, the theory of translation teaches us, as does the
theory of communication and inter-cultural activity, that one cannot really
translate without taking account of the context, or using the context to
deduce guidelines that are not linguistic themselves but do have an impact
on, and determine, lexical choices. In cases where these guidelines are not
easy to deduce, it would be sensible and helpful if they were stated explicitly. One never translates in a vacuum and each situation imposes
unavoidable constraints on the translator.

   Second, the same theory of translation highlights the active role that
those requesting and using translations will have to play, as partners in an
interactive process, by providing the translator not only with the text but
also with the means to grasp its context and take the appropriate decisions.

## Participation in Drafting Legislation

Let us now return to the issue that concerns us and try to draw some conclusions. The part translators are expected to play when translating legislative texts, as opposed to political texts, differs in only one respect and it can best be expressed as a tautology: to translate legislative texts, translators must take linguistic decisions with a legislative impact; to translate political texts, they must take linguistic decisions with a political impact.

The question may arise: are translators in some way to participate in the exercise of legislative power by translating texts? Do they participate in the wording of political messages by translating them? The answer, in my view, is affirmative! Translators should not underestimate the real impact of their work. There is a consensus on the need to change the perception of the translators' role from outside, which is often misguided and oversimplified. Translation is not just a simple business of languages; in the case of the EU it is a constituent part of the decision-making process that eventually becomes European policy and law.

I believe the importance of this subject would justify setting up the appropriate machinery to allow for two-way communication between all those who have a hand in drawing up legal and political texts – those who write the first language version and those who write the other language versions, namely the translators. Perhaps we should conclude that the term 'translator' does not measure up to a definition of our task in all its implications; that the legislator did choose the right word in the phrasing of Article 4 in Regulation No. 1; and that, to sum up, translation really does form a constituent part of the process of drafting multilingual texts. Perhaps one might decide there is a need for a new conceptual approach, one that gives a more accurate description of the translator's job and leads to a fairer division of responsibilities. To sum up: according to a widely held view, translation in an institutional setting is no more than a straightforward mechanical process, transferring text from one language to another with little thought involved. In this perception, it would be preferable for translators to do the translating, and leave the thinking to others. Fortunately for the EP translators, Parliament's Director-General and Director of Translation do not share that view, and I hope the debate will continue and will bear fruit.

### Acknowledgements

The writer would like to thank José Paulo Nascimento e Silva for a critical reading of the manuscript, Nicole Buchin for linguistic revision of the French original, Edward Seymour for the English translation and all the members of Working Group 2 for their patience and help.

## Notes

1. Regulation No. 1 determining the languages to be used by the European Economic Community (OJ 17, 6 June 1958, p. 385) and Regulation No. 1 determining the languages to be used by the European Atomic Energy Community (OJ 17, 6 June 1958, p. 401).
2. In this context see Yves Volman, Entre sémantique et pragmatique. Sens et équivalences des termes figurant dans les textes juridiques communautaires rédigés en plusieurs versions linguistiques [Between semantics and pragmatics. Meaning and equivalences of terms in Community legal texts drafted in several language versions], Doctoral thesis for the European University Institute, 1993, pp. 63 et seq.
3. COM(97) 626 final. Brussels: European Commission.
4. PE 226.403/fin. paragraphs 10 and 11. European Parliament.

## References

Caillé, P.-F. (1967) Traduire, c'est choisir. *Babel* XIII (1), 7–13.

Ortega y Gasset, José (1970) Miseria y esplendor de la traducción. In *Obras Completas* (Vol. V (1933–41) (pp. 433–52). Madrid: Revista de Occidente.

Snell-Hornby, Mary (1988) *Translation Studies. An Integrated Approach* (pp. 16 et seq.). Amsterdam/Philadelphia: John Benjamins.

*Chapter 5*

# European Affairs: The Writer, the Translator and the Reader

ARTURO TOSI

## The Evolution of our Translation Culture

### Pre-linguistics phases

Our understanding of translation problems today can greatly benefit from the diverse perceptions of the aims and challenges of translation in different cultures. The most influential discussions on translation theory and practice today begin with a reconstruction of our translation culture since its origin (Steiner, 1975; Bassnet-McGuire, 1980; Ballard, 1995). In spite of the conventional nature of any compartmentalisation that deals with the dynamic system of human culture, the quadripartite division proposed by Steiner has survived with merits that are instructive for both the theoretician and the practitioner.

The first phase embraces centuries from 300 BC when Romans took on many features of Greek culture, through to the Middle Ages when the West came into contact with Islam, and to the end of the 18th century, when the increasing amount of literary and non-literary translation work led to the publication of the first systematic study on the principles of translation (Tytler, 1790). The focus of this phase is on practical aspects, and its early analysts are identified in Horace and Cicero whose work gave us the first evidence of awareness of the major challenges of translation. This is also the time when translators begin to sign their work, perhaps reflecting not only the professional challenge in the creation of the new text but also the dilemma between the literal translation option and the equivalent-effect alternative. The concern that the limits of translation function as a burden on the personal re-creation of the translator is very clearly expressed by Horace in his *Ars Poetica*, where he states quite explicitly that no-one can translate both literally and well. The next centuries revisited the conflict between free and literal translation, with contributions which ranged from

45

that of St Jerome (400) to that of Luther (1530), all favouring colloquial and natural renderings until Tytler's suggestion that a good translation is one in which most of the original work is so completely transfused into another language as to be as strongly felt by a native of the country to which that language belongs, as it is by those speaking the language of the original work.

In Steiner's periodisation the second phase is characterised as a period of theory and hermeneutic enquiry. This period develops through the 19th century, when some of the modern methods and terminologies for approaching translation emerged, although the fundamental opposition remained unresolved, as Goethe (1826) poignantly commented when he referred to the contradiction between the inherent impossibility and absolutely necessity of translation. In this phase translation functions essentially as a one-way means of communication between prominent men of letters and their educated readers abroad. Typically under discussion are the methods of literary translation, from the early suggestion of a simple and noble style for translating Homer (Arnold, 1861) to Paul Valery's reservations about literary translation, especially of poetry (see Newmark, 1976). Significant is Benjamin's position (1923), which concludes this period. Focusing on literary and religious texts, he presents translation as the operation filling the gaps in meaning in a universal language. Unsurprisingly, Benjamin recommends literal translation and preservation of word-order, rejecting any consideration for the receiver's viewpoint.

Steiner's divisions include two simultaneous phases, the third and fourth, the former of which begins with the publication of the first papers on machine translation in the 1940s. The latter is marked by 'a reversion to the hermeneutic' approach, with enquiries from different disciplinary perspectives into the nature of texts, and with linguists making an attempt to distinguish types or the quality of texts. The 20th century has been called the age of translation, and not only because of the increase in world communication which has correspondingly increased the requirements for translation. There are also international agreements, documents and legislation between states, public and private organisations, which need to be translated for all the interested parties. All these give translation enhanced political importance, which is marked by the increasing attention paid to the perception of the receiver and the re-emergence of the fundamental conflict between the literal principle versus the equivalent effect. The end of the old period is marked by Matthew Arnold's landmark statement (1861) that one cannot achieve equivalent effect in translating Homer, as one knows nothing about his audiences. The new period – which places translation theory and practice in the wider context of communication – starts in the second half of the 19th century. This phase benefits not only from the exponential increase in technology; it also witnesses an unprecedented level of collaboration between the linguistic disciplines and other social sciences. This collaboration has led to a crucial re-examination of the role of the translator as communicator and a better understanding of translation work as a contribution to the development of national languages.

## The impact of machine translation

The optimistic view that machine translation would be able to provide the final answer to translation problems developed from the welcome collaboration between the humanities and technology, translation having long been dominated by the former. This optimism was also promoted by new needs for a wider range of texts to be translated, which gradually modified the perception of translation from that of a craft to that of a product. Certainly, the increase in the volume of translation since the end of the Second World War and, in particular in the last quarter of the 20th century, is evidence not only of the new 'international' age of western culture but also of the irreversible globalisation of the economy.

The early arguments expressed in relation to mechanical translation reflected the views of two sectors of specialists. The technologists emphasised the desirable economy of the new approach, while the humanists deplored the possible deterioration of human languages once they were operated mechanically. Following the early conflict, some remarkable progress was made as a result of the rapidly developing computer technology that would soon allow the gigantic memory of the artificial brain to move at supersonic speed. A further advance in the development of mechanical translation was marked by a more realistic re-definition of its function, which focused on texts in specific scientific and technical domains, while de-emphasising its contribution to the area of literary and social texts or even interpersonal relations. From the early stages, the developmental work involving linguists and technicians concentrated on language pairs, originally for specific purposes, but soon expanded to embrace all aspects of translation. The idea that one pivot or metalanguage could function as a common denominator emerged much later.

Since then, the major inconvenience has been the time and effort spent on establishing correlations and equivalences across language systems which could satisfy the largest possible number of contextual situations. Accordingly, the quality of language pairs varies considerably, depending on the stage of development reached. In the USA major efforts went into mechanical translation from Russian into English, whereas in Europe the most reliable and the most widely used pairs are French into English, English into French and French into Italian. Later the development of English into Italian proved to be comparatively easy due to the similarities between the Italian and French systems. This is because the source English lexicon used for the English–French pair could also be used for the development of the English–Italian pair. Among other languages, Spanish–French and French–Spanish have proved easy to develop following the French–Italian model, whereas any combination involving Romance and non-Romance languages, such as Dutch–Italian and especially any Romance language and German, has proved extremely difficult and the quality of the outcome is not comparable to that of other pairs. This is due to different word order as well as other major non-correlations of a syntactical nature.

The European Commission has been developing the Systran machine translation system since 1976. The system can produce 2000 pages of new translation per hour. There is, however, the catch that the new translation needs further processing by human intelligence if it is to be used for more than a rapid scan. This system can be adopted as a rapid information scanner to communicate the substance of a document when the source language is unknown to the reader. Why mechanical translation still struggles, given these limits and the substantial labour and expense invested in its development, is still a matter of controversy. Some argue that the reason why artificial intelligence (that can already cope with the most complex mathematical operations) is much slower in achieving accuracy in mechanical translation is due to the elusive nature of language. Given this, the promise is that new investment in development will expand the power of artificial intelligence in decoding, reading and understanding an ever-growing number of specific features. Others deeply disagree with this view and emphasise the glossary nature of the memory on which mechanical operation depends. They argue that such glossaries may speed up the laborious process of the translation of scientific and technological documents, but they do not translate a body of normal linguistic material into a parallel body in another language. In this sense they are aids to human translation, but machine translation will never achieve the appropriate determination of meaning, because of the different architecture of the human brain and artificial intelligence: one can recognise contexts, the other cannot and possibly will never be able to. In 1964 the American Philosophical Society (quoted in Steiner, 1975) issued a statement that is still relevant today: 'Work in machine translation has come up against a semantic barrier ... We have come face to face with the realisation that we will only have adequate mechanical translation when the machine can "understand" what it is translating'. Today after 35 years of technological advance and the microchip revolution, with machines capable of storing millions of megabytes of data more than the human brain, machines can read texts, but it still takes the human brain to understand them.

## Multidisciplinarity

In a much-quoted statement Newmark (1976) suggests that the main reason for formulating a translation theory, for proposing methods of translation related to and derived from it, for teaching translation and for translation courses is the appalling quality of so many published translations. If literary and non-literary translations without mistakes are rare, according to Newmark (1991) the translator of non-literary texts more often than not has to work on inaccurate and poorly written texts. The need to agree on general principles is underlined by Newmark and he stresses the urgency to investigate the subject at a time when accurate translation has become politically important. Since machine translation now exists and has demonstrated its usefulness and cost-effectiveness in some specific areas, the investigation of the theory and practice of translation has expanded its field of enquiry with the contribution of different disciplines. Under literary translations Steiner (1975) lists classical philosophy and comparative literature, lexical statistics and ethnography, the sociological study of class-speech, formal rhetoric, poetics and the study of grammar. Newmark (1976), who examines the relationship between non-literary translation and other disciplines, includes comparative linguistics, semantics, sociolinguistics, semiotics, pragmatics and textual criticism.

It is interesting, says Newmark, that the most recent works in translation studies of non-literary nature de-emphasise the activity of translation as an art and emphasise the role of the translator as a communicator. He recalls that semantics is the study of language in context; sociolinguistics investigates the problems of languages in contact, semiotics studies the meaning of signs in accordance between the receiver and interpretant; pragmatics is particularly sensitive to political communication; textual criticism enables the translator to interpret the text before s/he decides how to translate it.

The last ten years have witnessed an even more dramatic rejection of traditional oppositions such as 'faithful' versus 'beautiful', 'free' versus 'literal' translation or 'form' versus 'content', with a subsequent re-adjustment of the focus, from the subjective quality of the translator to the more objective constraints of the text. Some fundamental notions have been introduced by this multidisciplinary collaboration, which describes the new role of the translator as communicator as a person who should be able to discriminate between the pragmatic dimensions of the context, who should be conscious of the semiotic function of the context as well as the type of focus of the text, and who should then be able to design the new text structure in translation with the necessary sensitivity for discourse texture in the target language (Hatim & Mason, 1990, 1997). While there is a much wider and more sophisticated range of pragmatic instruments and guidelines available to the translator as communicator, many questions concerning the translator as a mediator, and the difficulties of translating between remote cultures, are still open. This is possibly because 'cultures' are difficult to define even in an age of 'international' culture, as their interpenetration is continual and dynamic.

In his contribution to this book Trim reminds us that no sector of European society is exempt from the effects of economic, political, social and cultural globalisation. He subsequently describes the challenge of an unprecedented volume of international loan-traffic, which especially concerns the novel dimension of our common culture – European affairs, legislation, politics. To make this international situation even more complex, European languages are developing new internal diversifications within the boundaries of their national communities. This is the result of living in what we call a mass society. The language for political communication differs from that of public administration, the language of public administration differs from that of advertisements and commercials, and so on. Not only do these varieties differ within the same national language, they vary substantially in different Member States. If we literally translate the political discourse that functions in one national tradition into the language of another Member State, it produces effects that may range from the meaningless to the ridiculous. These are quite simply the consequences of economic and political internationalisation in a society which is committed to remaining linguistically and culturally diverse. The private sector has become aware of the importance of the rules of communication and, in some cases, it has taken appropriate action. Many of us still remember when in the mid 1960s the multinational oil companies needed to prepare the public for a major increase in the price of petrol in Europe. Esso came up with the memorable slogan:

> I've got a tiger in my tank

| In German it became | 'Tu den Tiger in den Tank'; |
| in Spanish | 'Mete un tigre en el tanque'; |
| in Italian | 'Metti un tigre nel motore'; and |
| in French | 'Mettez un tigre dans votre moteur'. |

Clearly alternative translations like:

> 'Put a tiger in your engine'    or
> 'J'ai un tigre dans mon reservoir'

would have sounded strange to the international community of drivers, who needed to be told tactfully that cheap petrol was no longer available.

This digression leads me to put forward a preliminary consideration in connection with the reception of European discourse – before I turn to its analysis – a consideration regarding the evaluation of our translation culture. The phase in which translators believed in universally acceptable 'correct' communication is over. Since the current emphasis is rightly on communication, this means that attention will need to be placed on the receiver, who had been ignored previously. This new principle allows for a wide range of considerations, such as the pragmatic–semiotic dimensions of the context, the author's intentions, the text structure: all these are relevant to the analysis of the norms that characterise the style and structure of European discourse, as it appears in the texts that are translated in the Commission and Parliament. The distinction between the diverse types of European texts is also relevant to the decisions to be made by the translators and this is an issue that is explored in detail elsewhere in this book. Several questions of principle arise, however, in the conclusion of this brief survey of our translation culture: and these are relevant in the wider debate on language contacts and European multilingualism. If the writer of the original has deviated from the language norms of the type of text s/he has written, can the decision of the translator be different – whether it is a discussion paper, a report or a legislative document? Moreover, EU translators usually know the foreign language so well that they can determine the extent to which the text deviates from the language norms usually used in that topic on that type of occasion. Thus, the gap between the role of the EU translator as a communicator and as mediator is illustrated by the problematic decision as to whether and when s/he should be allowed to intervene in a text's grammatical or semantic oddness and to decide to normalise the text for the benefit of the receiver.

## European Multilingualism and Its New Challenges

### Language policy and Translation Service

Today over 350 million Europeans live in a federation of 15 Member States that has evolved into the current Union from previous collaborative frameworks such as the ECSC (European Coal and Steel Communities, 1951), the EURATOM (European Atomic Energy Communities, 1957) and the EEC (European Economic Communities, 1957). The Maastricht Treaty (1992) intensified the political nature of the collaboration, and it also endorsed the fundamental principles of the original federation. These were: (1) to respect the political sovereignty of each Member State, (2) to treat cultural diversity as one of Europe's major assets and (3) to maintain European multilingualism and to promote the different national languages.

The Union's legislation must be published in all the Member States' official languages before it becomes national law. Long before proposals

## The Community's Language Charter

Council Regulation No. 1 determining the languages to be used
by the European Economic Community (as amended)

THE COUNCIL OF THE EUROPEAN ECONOMIC COMMUNITY

Having regard to Article 217 of the Treaty which provides that the rules
governing the languages of the institutions of the Community shall,
without prejudice to the provisions contained in the rules of proceedings
of the Court of Justice, be determined by the Council, acting unani-
mously:

Whereas each of the nine languages in which the Treaty is drafted is
recognised as an official language in one or more of the Member State of
the Community.

HAS ADOPTED THIS REGULATION:

*Article 1*

The official languages and the working languages of the institutions of
the Community shall be Danish, Dutch, English, French, German, Greek,
Italian, Portuguese and Spanish.

*Article 2*

Documents which a Member State or a person subject to the jurisdiction
of a Member State sends to institutions of the Community may be drafted
in any one of the official languages selected by the sender. The reply shall
be drafted in the same language.

*Article 3*

Documents which an institution of the Community sends to a Member
State or to a person subject to the jurisdiction of a Member State shall be
drafted in the language of such State.

*Article 4*

Regulations and other documents of general application shall be drafted
in the nine official languages.

*Article 5*

The *Official Journal of the European Communities* shall be published in the
nine official languages.

---

*Article 6*

The institutions of the Community may stipulate in their rules of procedure which of the languages are to be used in specific cases.

*Article 7*

The languages to be used in the proceedings of the Court of Justice shall be laid down in its rules of procedure.

*Article 8*

If a Member State has more than one official language, the language to be used shall, at the request of such State, be governed by the general rules of its law.

This Regulation shall be binding in its entirety and directly applicable in all Member States.

---

**Figure 1** The Community's Language Charter

become national law, the European Commission (1994), the executive body of the Union, ensures that proposals can be widely discussed at all levels – European, national and local – in forms accessible to non-linguists and non-diplomats. For this reason, it was decided from the very outset that the official languages would be those of all Member States. The Community's Language Charter, Regulation No. 1, was developed in 1958 and amended as new states joined (see Figure 1).

The EU at present uses 11 languages, all Member States speaking their own principal tongue on equal terms, and it is considering admitting other countries including those once behind the iron curtain (for example Hungary, Poland and the Czech Republic). Every time the Union grows, so does the number of translators and interpreters. More languages mean more work, which costs more money and, at a time of rationalisation of resources, this has led managers to need to look for long-term solutions of the kind that can safeguard the principle of full multilingualism while setting the patterns for future enlargements. Technical measures and modern technology sometimes seem to come to the rescue.

## The Historic Momentum

Although an increasing number of people now know more than one European language, the Union still relies heavily on its different national languages for communications between a significant proportion of Europeans; this is because we value our national languages both as a symbol of our national identity and as a source of cultural enrichment. European communication via national languages must therefore reflect that this ambition is realistic and attainable, and that the use of different languages to communicate with European citizens is not impossible but is clear evidence of our ability to master modern technologies for the purpose of crossing barriers and bridging cultures.

The single most important technological innovation, sometimes adopted to limit the cost of translation, comes from the use of machine translation. Computers have already been proven to function as ancillary tools, providing databanks to assist translators and other Union staff in their search for equivalent terms in the official languages. Similarly, specialised glossaries are produced for the main areas of Union activities, in an attempt to identify the topics of particular interest at any given time and to collect, study, harmonise and publish the terminology used in Union texts. Professional translators, however, are very well aware that it is impossible even for the most advanced machine to understand the full implications of a text, and that human intervention is always necessary to ascertain whether a computer-assisted translation does or does not make sense and if it gives the 'right' interpretation.

In the Commission not all translation work is directed towards producing legislation, rather it covers a wide range of

> speeches and speaking notes, briefings and press releases, international agreements, policy statements, answers to written and oral parliamentary questions, technical studies, financial reports, minutes, internal administrative matters and staff information, scripts and captions for films and other promotional material, correspondence with ministries, films, pressure groups and individuals, and publications of every size and format on a huge range of topics for opinion-formers and the general public. (European Commission, 1994)

In the European Parliament, though not in the Commission, all languages are used as working languages and can be either source or target language, depending on the circumstances. Documents are, however, increasingly *drafted* in a small number of languages (69% in English and French, 87% in English, French, German and Spanish) but there is almost perfect equality in the number of *translated* texts – around 9% for each of the languages (Wilson, 1997).

The unequal use of official languages effectively means that a very large proportion of the work carried out in the Commission and Parliament, before it becomes *translated* into the languages of all Member States, is *drafted* in one of four working languages (French, English, German and

Spanish). Of the two dominant working languages French tends to be used especially for internal staff regulations and management of the offices, as it is also the language of the local environment and administration. English is increasingly used to draft consultative papers, working documents and other publications on most topics of social, political and economic interest for the general public. This massive enterprise has recently attracted attention in terms of operation costs, but also in connection with the quality of the translations which bring the decisions, the voice and ultimately the image of the Europe to each Member State. Ordinary citizens, who do not have any specific concern with language policy and translation problems, simply wish to be fully informed about their rights and duties as Europeans, which is a prerequisite for democratic participation at all levels of European affairs. Significantly, increased emphasis is on communication: 'European Citizens First' states a new EU programme for the professionalisation of all services, and this has become a priority in the programme of the present Secretary General, Romano Prodi (1999). Accordingly, translators feel that they are, first and foremost, mediators between the various national languages, which have developed over the centuries as vehicles of specific national cultures, and the new supranational dimension – of economic, social, political and juridical nature – of the European Union.

## The European Dimension and Language Contacts

### The translator as mediator

Awareness that the quality of translations can vary according to external circumstances, which are often independent of the professionalism of the largest multilingual service in the world, has sparked many discussions within the EU Translation Service. The Service increasingly monitors the work of its outside freelance translators, who are often called upon to cope with certain languages in highly specialised fields or who are brought in to relieve the pressure of the workload, which can increase suddenly in response to political imperatives. As the quality required is high, and the translations will have to stand on their own as original documents, access to terminology and documentary resources is constantly available, together with the name of a contact who can assist with translating problems. Within this framework of support the intention of the Commission is to provide as much help as possible, yet it does acknowledge that the inner workings of the Community often make use, and require the knowledge, of an inside jargon.

There has also been much discussion within the Translation Services on the origin of 'Eurospeak' and how all the languages can best be protected from contamination through this jargon which, according to some, seems to derive especially from English. The dominant argument is that the 'de-generation' of this language is due to its use as lingua franca by European officials who are not native-speakers, and often do not have, and never have had, a great deal of contact with either British or American culture. French is in a similar position but many translators argue that it is protected by everyday interaction with the French-speaking community in Brussels and Luxembourg. Hence the widespread view that the best way to protect European languages from contamination, in the multilingual environment of the EU headquarters, is to refer repeatedly to their 'good use' in the natural context of each Member State.

Various steps are taken to ensure that this happens. A high-quality service is maintained, above all through very selective recruitment, followed by facilities for pre-service and in-service training, regular sessions with experts in linguistics, translation and in specific fields of language use, as well as periods of leave in the country into whose language translators are specialised to translate. In spite of this intensive agenda, the challenges emerging from new supranational European experiences bring to the desks of translators a variety of linguistic dilemmas, which range from unusual lexical items of everyday life, to difficult adaptations of juridical terms to fit the legal system of a Member State, where the same notions do not exist. All Translation Units are actively involved in both external and internal consultations to overcome these problems. Increasingly they feel that national usage cannot come to the rescue and thus they opt for literal translations that secure linguistic and cultural integrity though not necessarily clarity and understanding.

The debate on the role of the translator as mediator is, however, growing rapidly, not only because of the status held by texts published by the EU but also because EU translators are well aware of the additional responsibility they have, compared to their colleagues in the Interpretation Service. Their role as language innovators, they argue, is not sufficiently acknowledged in EU political quarters. Above all, there is the fact that in the EU multilingual environment the translators, who deal with the written rather than the spoken language, set models and change trends. This is exactly the opposite of what happens in a monolingual situation in the national communities where changes are generally adopted in writing long after they have been used and accepted in the spoken language.

In the last ten years the debate about *Eurospeak* or *Europese* has been a lively one, with language-specific newsletters and the multilingual periodical *Terminologie et Traduction*, as well as seminars with guest speakers, including specialist lexicographers promoting, and more often discouraging, innovative lexical choices. The focal point of the debate is the quest for the 'correct' translation, whether the term of reference is the 'good use' sought from the outside expert or the 'right equivalent' stipulated by an official authority. The national versions of the Official Journal of the European Communities has a large repertoire of (1) foreign words that translators eventually decided to include in the official legal texts followed by (2) paraphrases in the national languages.

When, however, translations present problems that may have juridical implications, translators are usually referred to the appropriate national authority, either the Ministry of Foreign Affairs or the Ministry of Justice, as in the examples of Italian translations given here.

| | | |
|---|---|---|
| Republic of Estonia | ≡ | *Repubblica Estone* (not *Repubblica di Estonia* or *dell'Estonia*) |
| concubinage | ≡ | *convivenza more uxorio* (not *concubinato*) |
| lobbying | ≡ | *lobbismo* (not *lobby, lobbies* or *lobbying*) |
| law enforcement agency | ≡ | *autorità di polizia* or *autorità incaricata* |

Transpositions of idioms and metaphors that are well rooted in a foreign culture seem less controversial, possibly because the translators see themselves less as innovators in this domain, since journalists and reporters lead the way in most European languages as regards the present international jargon of politics and administration which is largely dominated by English. See these Italian examples:

| | | |
|---|---|---|
| the long wave of | – | *l'onda lunga del* |
| to be wearing a different hat | – | *mettersi un cappello diverso* |
| tailor made | – | *tagliato su misura* |
| high profile and low profile | – | *alto profilo e basso profilo* |

While the same figures of speech now dominate multilingual communications in EU quarters, the debate on how to 'bend' the European texts for readers in the national communities has contrasted puristic versus innovative positions, striving to find or to endorse the 'correct' translation. But the most recent seminars and workshops held within the Commission and Parliament, however, pointed out that this debate is in danger of degenerating into a vicious circle: readers have problems understanding EU materials, authors criticise the translations and the translators complain about the original texts. The conclusion was that a way forward must be found (Tosi, 2001).

## Language Standardisation and National Attitudes

The same message seems to emerge from any consultation which adopts the perspective that a true understanding of the full implications of translating in a multilingual environment necessitates a move away from the generalisation that Eurospeak is generated by poor English usage in non-mother tongue contexts. Trim in his contribution argues further that interpenetration between languages and cultures in contact, mediated by plurilingual speakers, is by no means new. Perhaps, the question arises, he says, of whether this process is an inevitable development, changing but enriching rather than impoverishing the languages concerned; or whether it is a threat to their linguistic and cultural integrity to be monitored, controlled and, where possible, resisted.

It is interesting to examine the implications of the interpenetration mechanisms described by Trim, in the reception of EU materials in some national contexts where readers are accustomed to foreign borrowings, and yet may be utterly unable to understand a text. In Italy, for example, outside the group of diplomats, politicians and other specialist users, some of the most regular readers of European affairs are school teachers. In 1997 a conference in Turin (UCIIM, 1997) brought together school teachers and university teachers, as they had a common interest in language, education and European citizenship. A group of teachers from an urban multi-ethnic area reported on a major Socrates-funded project designed to introduce a European dimension into the school curriculum from primary to secondary school. Primary teachers were using posters and maps of Europe, with coloured tables and statistics on different religions, languages, ethnic origins, to illustrate to their pupils that the diversity in their classroom was just a microcosm of European society at large. A group of middle-school teachers of foreign languages were training their pupils to plan a trip abroad, and were making an application to gain EU funds for travel and expenses. A team of secondary-school teachers of history reported on a project concerned with the planning of human resources in Europe. They had chosen to read to their pupils the Italian version of Mme Cresson's famous White Paper: *Teaching and Learning: Towards the Learning Society* (1996). All the teachers admitted that they themselves (let alone their pupils) had had serious problems understanding these documents in the Italian language, including some of the most basic information, even the titles.

Why did these teachers reading Italian materials published by the Union report such disorientation? Their reports indicated, first, that the sentence structure tended to complicate rather than facilitate the interpretation of the content. The lexical choice was also identified as frequently being unusual in the national context within those specific topical or professional domains. As many teachers complained, the documents were found to be understandable only to those readers who were (a) knowledgeable about the topic in question and (b) able to read (between the lines of the Italian text) the French or English that was the source of the Italian translation. Why is it that in Italy we seem to report more problems of comprehension than requests to defend the integrity of our national language? Let me try to summarise the Italian sociolinguistic situation which, I believe, is fairly evident to anyone travelling through Italy.

The peculiar historical development of this country, and its late political unification, have given to us some of the most beautiful cities in Europe, the small capitals of old independent city states. This process was responsible for the century-long regionalisation of our languages and cultures. Late in the history of Europe we achieved a common national language. This point can be summarised in the technical statement that today the Italian language is still not really standardised. We should be careful with this word 'standardised', as in French the meaning of 'standard' in ordinary everyday language does not match the meaning of 'standard' in English, as we find it in the technical expression 'standard language'. How can I put it in different words? Compared to other European languages, Italian is not a very standardised language, in that there is still little agreement between *'signifiant et signifié'* amongst its native speakers. The historical reason for this lies in the decentralisation of our culture, which has given the Italian language a wealth of words and forms, which were not only the resources of our literary tradition but also sources of endless disagreement in our political life and public administration. Two examples will suffice.

In the 19th century a sensitive poet, Giacomo Leopardi, said that 'the more vague and imprecise language is, the more poetic it becomes'. More or less at the same time, the Italian Prime Minister Giovanni Giolitti (1841–1928), now known as the inventor of Italian bureaucracy, was often heard to remark. 'The law must be applied to one's enemy and interpreted for one's friend'. Only a few years ago, one of our great modern writers, Italo Calvino (1984), reminded us that 'Italian is the only language in Europe in which the word *vago* (vague) means also "lovely, attractive", because the idea of uncertainty and indefiniteness is still associated with gracefulness and pleasure'.

Calvino was interested in translation and he believed that all European languages showed their limitations when it came to cultural relations and transfer. Italian in particular, he said, was handicapped by a lack of codification, because the majority of Italians wrote mixing various codes, 'borrowing words and accumulating terms of the most diverse origins, which then develop special Italian roots, so that those who use them move from their domestic to international meaning, playing on finesse and ambiguity' (Calvino, 1965). Calvino, writing on the difference between Italian and other European languages, highlighted the fact that the advantage of a 'vague' language was to increase the scope for the translation of literature, but in a non-literary texts its vagueness was a distinct disadvantage. A linguist, an expert on translation (Newmark, 1976), made the distinction that when translation needs to function as a science rather than as an art, approximation is limiting and the less a language is standardised the more it is penalised.

If we now return to our original question of the comprehension of a European discourse in different national contexts, I think that perhaps there is a lesson to be learnt from the Italian situation I have just described. Because of its limited standardisation, the extreme Italian situation reveals only the tip of an iceberg; an iceberg before which the Titanic volume of European communications is currently growing. Once Member States realise that the problem is not one of linguistic purism, and that the discussion will no longer concern the correction of a few lexical items, more and more people may find it objectionable to live in an unnecessarily diglossic situation: that is to say that besides the variety of the national language, expressing the meanings of the national culture, there will be another variety – a sort of (all-embracing) high-level interlanguage – into which many Member States will need to render an immediate translation of everything which is said in other European languages and particularly English.

If the gulf between the political discourse used by the media in Italy and that used in other countries seems to be becoming wider, a similar phenomenon can be observed in other countries. However, the elicited concern is different in that it regards linguistic purity. In a country like France, for instance, many readers write to prestigious newspapers calling for drastic measures to protect their national language (*Le Monde*, 27 June 1998):

> Pourquoi, sinon par paresse, infléchir (déformer?) le sense du mot français *globalisation*, alors que *mondialisation* ou, à la rigueur, *planétarisation* conviennent parfaitement? Affublé de ce nouveau sens, *globalisation* est un anglicisme qui introduit une ambiguité (une polysémie inutile) dans notre langue et donc l'appauvrit au lieu de l'enrichir. Vive la '*mondialisation*'!

> (Why, if not for laziness, should we restrict (deform?) the meaning of the French word *globalisation* when *mondialisation* or, more precisely *planetarisation*, perfectly fit the bill? Warped by this new meaning, *globalisation* is an Anglicism and introduces an ambiguity ( an unnecessary polysemy) into our language, thus making it poorer, not richer. Vive la '*mondialisation*'!)

Benjamin (1923) states that translation goes beyond enriching the language and culture of a target-language country, beyond renewing and maturing the life of the original text, beyond expressing and analysing the most intimate relationship between languages, and becomes a way of entry into a universal language. Many Europeans, however, do not agree with this view, rather they express their outrage at the degradation of their national language, as we saw in France. In Britain, too, there are international deviations from 'proper' standard British use. But many people would say that in Britain public perception of the European influence on language content is often distorted by ideological, not linguistic factors. From these reactions it seems that an interesting pattern is about to emerge in Europe.

Specifically when the national language is not one of the drafting languages, and it is used more frequently as a target language than as a source of translation, and where public perception is not distorted by ideological factors, motivation to understand European discussions is high, even if there are more problems with the comprehension of EU translations. When, however, the national language is one of the drafting languages, and when public perception is divided on European issues, there can be alarming and puristic calls for the protection of the national language, even when there are fewer problems of comprehension.

## Emphasis on Good Communication

### Consensus as a prerequisite

There is a long path ahead if we are to develop an appropriate translation culture in support of European multilingualism, and no future scenario can be ruled out, as was pointed out by Eco in his recent *The Search for the Perfect Language* (1993). Like Eco, many European writers have made their predictions following a natural inclination to link old experiences to future developments. However, an analysis of the future cohabitation of languages which was representative of the challenges faced by European multilingualism today was made by Italo Calvino more than 30 years ago (1965).

Calvino was aware of the fact that historical circumstances were likely to threaten European languages and that their happy cohabitation – what today we call multilingualism – depended so much on their translatability. Italian, he said, was penalised on several grounds. Its vagueness and polymorphism were far more widespread than in other languages. What is more, specific Italian meanings develop around intellectual notions that international use tended to harmonise. But he also added:

> No language can be regarded as exactly meeting the needs of modern life: not French, German, Russian, Spanish – not even English (though for different reasons) . . . Our age is characterised by this contradiction:

on the one hand we need to be able to translate everything which is said into other languages immediately; on the other we realise that every language is a self-contained system of thought and by definition untranslatable.

Then he concluded:

My prediction is this: each language will revolve around two poles. One pole is immediate translatability into other languages, which will come close to a sort of all-embracing, high-level interlanguage; and another pole will be where the singular and secret essence of the language, which is by definition untranslatable, is distilled. (Calvino, 1965)

This process is already with us: we are witnesses to its development every day. In some countries – I am told – the diglossia has already been acknowledged, and some European documents, which have an official, almost incomprehensible translation, require a more popular version for ordinary readers. I am told that in Denmark there are already parallel official and popular versions of some European texts. Clearly this approach is not exportable everywhere, as we have different national expectations. But if we are to learn from collaboration, perhaps to identify common patterns, we need to start from a consensus established across our different perspectives. To my mind there are at least four different perspectives in this debate; they all deserve consideration and their different points of view need to be appreciated.

The first perspective is that of linguists, approaching language from an academic point of view. When they propose or challenge a theory, they do so with the intention of sharing their experience. Language scholars see language from a special angle, often with an eye to old experiences and future developments. But they are not lexicographers, and they usually prefer to side with the interests of the speakers rather than defend the purity of the language. However, communication in the modern world is neither a simple nor an obvious matter, even for academics. When we compare multilingualism today with similar phenomena in the past, we begin to see some differences, which suggest that our current understanding of this phenomenon will not always help us to predict future developments. Take language and culture contacts. In the past their outcome was determined by international relations among cultural élites or by the movement of migrant populations which brought individual speakers or large communities of speakers of different languages into contact. In both cases our national languages have been enriched by these exchanges; possibly because the interaction between the two related cultures always involved interaction between speakers. Today the rapid development of communication and information technologies, as well as the internationalisation of our exchanges, makes language contacts possible, sometimes necessary, even without cultural interaction between the speakers concerned. This is a feature of our technological era, and since no sector of European society is exempt from the effects of economic, political, social and cultural globalisation, today we are faced with the challenge of an unprecedented volume of international loan-word traffic, concerning all dimensions of European affairs and, more dramatically, those discussed in the article by Renato Correia.

The second perspective is that of professional translators who struggle with an increasing work load and tough deadlines, and for this reason are often pressed to make on the spot decisions, while always wishing they had the time to make more considered policy decisions. Under these circumstances it is not surprising if they feel that authors and receivers do not fully appreciate the translators' role as true innovators. Indeed their role as language innovators is little acknowledged by the dominant translation culture, which originates from the monolingual environment from which most MEPs hail. In such monolingual environments it is always the spoken language that innovates the written language; whereas in the multilingual environment of the European Parliament and Commission, exactly the opposite is true, as the linguistic decisions that are most binding are those of the translators, not those of the interpreters, who deal only with the spoken language.

The third perspective is that of those who have to make policy decisions concerning finance, quality control and rationalisation. Especially in view of future enlargements, this perspective is of great importance, as professional consensus is a prerequisite to give the right direction to political decisions for the preservation of full multilingualism.

The final perspective comes from those working in the field of modern technologies and artificial intelligence, which are playing an increasing role in the translation culture now widespread in EU circles. The crucial question is the size of the current gap separating human translators and machine translation; and whether this quality difference is likely to widen or narrow. The limits of human translation in the EU are explained by some of the in-house regulations imposed on translators, encouraging a word-by-word approach, as if each unit and stretch of language corresponded to the original and vice versa. This is why EU translators, whose professional standards are very high and who, unlike machines, are capable of understanding contextualised language, cannot make full use of their interpretative and creative skills required to 'bend' the EU texts towards the receivers' target language. Thus the widespread feeling among the profession today is that translators should reappropriate some of the rules of thumb of good cultural translation, which were not made available to them, possibly for historical reasons that are no longer politically justified. Newmark (1976) lists a number of such rules:

(1)   The translator should deal freely with the sentence and avoid reproduction of the original sequence by dealing with a word-for-word approach.

(2)   If the writing of the source language is poor it is normally the translator's duty to improve it.

(3)   All statements depend on presupposition, and where sentences are obscure or ambiguous, the translator must determine the presupposition and interpret any ambiguity.

(4)   The translator should reject obsolete, rare or one-off words, invented through interferences that appear in bilingual but not in monolingual dictionaries.

(5)   The translator should produce a different translation of the same word, idiom or even the same text for different types of audiences.

(6)   The translator has no right to create neologisms unless he or she is a member of an interlingual glossary team.

(7)   Modish words, internationalised by the media, predictable patterns and the fill-ins between stimulus and response that may appear in the source language should not be reproduced in the target language, although they may have their equally predictable equivalents.

(8)   The translator needs to be able to determine to what extent the text deviates from the language norms used in that topic on that type of occasion, and needs to take the initiative to normalise a badly written text.

(9)   The translator must distinguish synonyms used to give additional or complementary information from synonyms used simply to refer to a previously mentioned object or concept.

(10)  Punctuation, whatever the language, is such a specific convention, dealing with the expressive and communicative nature of the text, that it cannot be transferred across languages.

When the foundations of European multilingualism were laid in the Language Charter, politicians possibly took the view that there was only one 'correct' equivalent term in each language, a condition which often distinguishes a technical translations rather than those with a literary or cultural nature. The subsequent growth of European materials, including political statements, directives and publications for opinion-formers which are produced in EU quarters, reflect the increased integration of European activities in the past 40 years and the differences in cultures that must be taken into account in translation. Yet the limits imposed on independent initiatives by translators' free initiatives are the same as those for legal documents and this has tended to distance official EU communication from the languages of the national communities in Member States.

Today we still know little about the reception of the 'voice of Europe' in Member States. Is there a common pattern? Or are there different attitudes towards the internationalisation of political discourse, especially when it develops around a common European content? We are still far from being able to rely on a detailed and comprehensive picture, and there is strong consensus that this can only be achieved by formal measures being taken in different national communities to monitor the reception of EU documents. The main call is to maximise the translators' experience and to spread awareness of their innovative role among the people who are most concerned with European affairs.

There is another reason which justifies the introduction of such a monitoring structure. In the past we could assume that the receivers of EU texts remained a small élite of politicians and administrators: people who were usually well acquainted with European legislation, its political discourse and terminologies. Today we know that the texts and documents produced by the Union are used increasingly by a large public of readers, especially young people and professionals, who are convinced Europeans, who seek active participation in European affairs, and who certainly do not wish to be excluded from new European facilities and opportunities. This brings this article to its final point. The need to re-examine the translation culture of the Union, its foundation and effect is emphasised especially by the most active groups of committed Europeans. They increasingly realise that the chance to maintain political support for multilingualism in Europe may well depend ultimately on the ability to deliver legislation and texts, demonstrating that the content of European discussions and decisions can be translated effectively into EU national languages. Multilingualism, which is the essence of European diversity and the symbol of the richness of our cultural heritage, must not be allowed to build barriers across the language communities. This is why good and effective communication needs to become the priority, and if the European Translation Services – by definition bridge-builders – are allowed to adapt their methods and approaches to the new translation culture, they may well be able to overcome some of the major difficulties of the profession which are well summed up in Goethe's remark that translation is always 'essential' and 'impossible'.

## References

Arnold, M. (1861) On translating Homer and last words on translating Homer. In *Essays Literary and Critical*. London: Everyman, Dent.

Ballard, M. (1995) *De Cicero a Benjamin: Traductuers, Traductions, Reflexions*. Lille: Presse Universitaire de Lille.

Bassnet-McGuire, S. (1980) *Translation Studies*. London: Methuen.

Benjamin, W. (1923) The translator's task. In H. Arendts (ed.) (1970) *Illuminations*. London: Cape.

Calvino, I. (1965) L'italiano, una lingua tra le altre lingue. In *Rinascita* 5,XXII, January. Reprinted in *Una Pietra Sopra*. Torino: Einaudi, 116–26.

Calvino, I. (1984) *Lezioni Americane. Sei proposte per il Prossimo Millennio,* Torino: Einaudi, English translation (1988): *Six Memos for the Next Millennium*. Cambridge, MA: Harvard University Press.

Cresson, E. (1996) *Teaching and Learning. Towards the Learning Society* (Italian translation: *Insegnare e Apprendere: Verso la Società Conoscitiva*). Luxembourg: Office for Official Publications of the European Communities.

Eco, U. (1993), *The Search for the Perfect Language*. London: Harper Collins.

European Commission (1994) *A Mulilingual Community at Work*. Luxembourg Translation Service: Office for Official Publications of the European Communities

Goethe, J.W. (1826) *Samatliche Weke* 39. (Letter to Thomas Carlyle.)

Hatim, B. and Mason, I. (1990) *Discourse and the Translator*. London and New York: Longman.

Hatim, B. and Mason, I. (1997) *The Translator as Communicator*. London and New York: Routledge.

Newmark, P. (1976) The theory and craft of translation. *Language Teaching and Linguistics: Abstracts* (Jan.). Reprinted in V. Kinsella (ed.) (1978) *Language Teaching and Linguistics: Surveys* (pp. 79–100). Cambridge: Cambridge University Press.

Newmark, P. ( 1991) *About Translation*. Clevedon: Multilingual Matters.

Prodi, R. (1999) Intervention of Prof. Prodi in European Council, 3 June 1999.

Steiner, G. (1975), *After Babel. Aspects of Language and Translation*. Oxford: Oxford University Press.

Tosi, A. (2001) Lingua italiana e affari europei. Three interventions for the Italian Translation Service at the European Commission and Parliament, June. In A. Tosi (ed.) *La voce dell'Europa in traduzione multilingue*. Special issue of *Rivista Italiana di Psicolinguistica Applicata* Vol. 3, pp. 19–35, 37–54, 55–79.

Tosi, A. (2002) The Europeanisation of Italian language by the European Union. In A.L. Lepschy and A. Tosi (eds) *Multilingualism in Italy: Past and Present* (pp. 170–94). Oxford: Legenda.

Tytler, A. (1790) *Essay on the Principles of Translation*. London: Dent.

UCIIM (1997) Le lingue straniere e la formazione giuridico-economica del cittadino europeo. Conference organised by Unione Cattolica Insegnanti Italiani Medi e Società Editrice Italiana, Torino, 6–7.

Wilson, B. (1997), Report on the Translation Service of the European Parliament, Note to the Members of the Working Party on Multilingualism and Future Enlargements. Unpublished paper. Luxembourg.

## Chapter 6

# The Contribution of Freelance Translators

FREDDIE DE CORTE

The European Union's multilingualism reflects a historic and natural choice. Right from the start, the EU officially opted for linguistic diversity, an approach enshrined in the founding treaties since the creation of the first community for coal and steel.[1] With six official languages and 30 language combinations from the outset, institutional multilingualism was bound to cause problems for translation and interpretation, particularly regarding finding properly qualified professionals: there was no special training for either translators or interpreters at the time. Even then, some said that the limit had been reached. Today, with 11 languages and 110 language combinations, we hear the same voices raised again. But what will be the practical consequences of the European Council decisions taken in Tampere in October 1999, and the accession of 12 extra Member States?

When the European Communities made their choice, they were clearly voicing a political determination to preserve, protect and promote multilingualism. They regarded it as the best way of binding together the citizens of the EU's Member States. Indeed, multilingualism is widely considered an asset; languages reflect their civilisations and make them intelligible. Languages and civilisations can enrich one another through mutual contact.

The EU's founding fathers were right to say that Europe is stronger if it speaks with a single voice. But that does not mean it should have to speak with a single language. Europe's linguistic complexity is a reflection of our extremely rich cultural heritage; and languages are an integral part of that. Indeed Europe has had a language policy since the very first treaties. However, the policy is not set in granite; it is changing with the pace of enlargement, the increase in European activity and the growth of the information society. These three developments have had one effect in common:

they have increased the cost of multilingualism and created a number of practical problems in terms of its organisation, planning and quality.

Several resolutions by MEPs (e.g. Mr Coppieters, Mr Colla and others in 1979 and 1981) have highlighted the problems raised by the multilingual option within Parliament. The Nyborg report[2] clarifies and explains Parliament's position in greater detail: Parliament is opposed to any restriction or unequal treatment of the European Communities' official languages. It supports the democratic right of MEPs to use their mother tongue both actively and passively, and insists that suitable measures be taken to reduce the problems to which this requirement gives rise.

From their first utterances, the European institutions decided to make use of the services of freelance translators, to ease the burden on their 'in-house' services. This cooperative policy has changed over the years, for political and organisational reasons. Like the multilingualism of the European institutions themselves, freelance translation can be seen from various points of view – the political, organisational, legal, financial, to mention some of the most important. In this article I shall confine my remarks to the linguistic aspects: I propose to comment on the linguistic aspect of freelance translation and multilingualism within the EU.

Consequently I shall not dwell on the issue of whether the institutions should be using freelance translators, and if so to what extent. Freelance translation is now an integral part of the way in which the European institutions organise their work. Nor do I see any value in discussing the view that is sometimes heard that 'there are no good freelance translators'; such a generalisation speaks of arrogance and ignorance. We all know that some freelance translators are excellent. Indeed, the ability of independent freelancers to survive for many years in an increasingly competitive market demonstrates that their quality is not in doubt. It is hence only natural that good freelance translators can command a high price. The question is whether the institutions are prepared to pay for quality.

Working with freelance translators means that the European institutions must apply strict standards in terms of quality, integrity, price structure, coordination and availability. Such criteria should appear in the specifications for Community invitations to tender. In the case of translation agencies, of which the institutions are making increasing use for financial reasons, it is essential to find a solution to the problem of the failure of certain agencies that fail to provide any guarantee of quality. Most of these are not members of any professional association and thus evade the quality standard, which such associations lay down, with their professional codes for technical proficiency and integrity. At the lower end of the market, such standards are often rather lax. The agencies with the best reputations provide greater guarantees of quality because they demand rather more stringent standards from their freelancers.

The freelance translators' contribution to the work of the European institutions and the translation process can be discerned from various points of view. The freelance translator, who is at the centre of the conflict between standardisation and destandardisation, globalisation and national or even regional awareness, has a special role to play. Consideration of the linguistic impact of freelance translation needs to take into account several aspects and their links with globalisation and European integration.

The linguistic impact of freelance translators derives directly from their position as a bridge between the institutions for which they work and the outside world, especially their country of origin. They have an advantage over civil service translators who, with a few exceptions (notably those working in Brussels), no longer live in their country of origin. Freelance translators provide an additional dimension to the work of translation in the European institutions because, unlike EU civil servants, they are in direct contact with the living language and culture of their country of origin. Translator officials living abroad risk losing contact with national or regional reality and the creative and evolutionary development of their language. Where there is such contact its effect will invariably be delayed. Their mother tongue's grammatical structures gradually begin to blur and the language loses its depth and expressive capacity, bringing to mind George Orwell's 'Newspeak'.

Freelance translators can help civil service translators to face the very real risks that a standardised language policy would create. These risks are the corollaries of globalisation and development of the information society. In this 'global village' individual and collective migration is becoming increasingly easy and frequent. The intensification of intercultural contact has many advantages, but also some serious disadvantages: it brings with it an enriching multilingualism and the positive effects of uni- and multidirectional interference; but it not only creates, it also destroys languages. The standardisation of language is almost bound to lead to an impoverishment of national languages, and hence of thought, culture and identity. The main risk is likely to derive from cultural colonisation by English, or rather – even more to be feared if that were possible – 'World English', that sometimes grotesque form of the language that everyone seems to understand and speak and which some unfortunately regard as the only possible form of international communication. The English language itself is likely to be the first casualty.

There are others. Since Austria joined the EU, the Austrian variant has tended to be expelled by German equivalents in European documents: 'Jänner' (January) is replaced by 'Januar', for instance. In many cases the damage is fairly limited, but the effects of standardisation are much more serious and lead to the loss of culturemes. Yet I do not agree with the defeatist view that the national languages – particularly 'small languages' such as Dutch – will disappear within the space of a few decades, due to the colonising force of English. On the contrary, our smaller languages are full of life and are increasingly resistant to invasion by the larger languages.3

However, even the largest and most widely used language can die out, as Latin or Copt has shown. We must all, whether we are 'message producers' (MEPs and administrators) or 'message conveyors' (translators, interpreters and terminologists) remain alert and continue to fight for our respective mother tongues; they must not be sacrificed in the name of efficiency.

Freelance translators can help us to protect our respective national languages from abusive language borrowing. This is a normal consequence of contact between languages. There have always been borrowings and there always will be. What has changed is their number and the frequency with which they have latterly been entering any given language. In so far as a borrowing serves to fill a lexical gap, it enriches the language. But there is a risk in an overly lax attitude, which ceases to search for the indigenous term or turn of phrase but merely repeats the word used in the source text (often French or English), with the excuse that the message readers are insiders and will understand. Contamination of this kind clearly leads to an impoverishment of the national languages. Freelance translators can instil fresh life into the 'eurolect',4 the language of the European institutions. The emergence of the eurolect is inevitable in that the legal system set up by the Treaties requires a specific Community language.[5] It is the result of the hybridisation of national languages, mainly at the lexical level .

The phenomenon of neology is extremely important not only for the renewal of our national languages but also for the creation of the eurolect. Many neologisms have enriched our languages over the years. They have mainly been sense neologisms, such as 'directive' or 'community'; syntagmatic neologisms, such as 'democratic deficit'; borrowings; acronyms, such as 'Socrates' (System for Organizing Content to Review And Teach Educational Subjects) or 'Erasmus' (EuRopean Community Action Scheme for the Mobility of University Students); calques; or neologisms involving a change of register, as in the French phrase 'plancher sur un dossier', in which 'plancher' – student slang for 'being questioned in front of the class' – has moved to a higher register to mean 'making a public speech on a certain subject'. As far as the eurolect – and all the other '-lects' – are concerned, neology is generally in the hands of professionals in the various industries and, only to a lesser extent in those of the institutions' linguists. The situation has occasionally caused proof-reading problems.

Some neologisms have entered the national language used in the European institutions despite their failure to respect the morphology of the language. Thus in Italian, 'comitologia' ought to be replaced by the more authentic form 'comitatologia'. In the case of the national languages, neologisms often reach the European institutions through the intermediary of free-lance translators. The message producers and message conveyors may then pick them up, establishing the neologisms concerned in their respective mother tongues.

Although freelance translators contribute to the renewal of the various national languages in the EU institutions, by the same token they also act as linguistic scavengers. Through their direct contact with the living language they can often use their translation work for the institutions to speed up the interment of linguistic cadavers: archaic words and turns of phrase which linguists thought had long since fallen into disuse, but which resurface from time to time in the translations of the European institutions. Freelance translators also have an impact on style. As politics is gradually opening up, becoming more democratic and transparent, so the language of politicians is slowly but surely adapting to the new canons of readability. Since Community law is a common standard, a compromise between different cultures and traditions, legislative documents (but also, alas, information leaflets) are worded in a stiff, artificial and hermetic style. It gives rise to a pompous and unnecessarily complicated idiom that is plainly unsuited to the purpose of communication. 'Officialese' of this kind in Italian, for example, replaces the normal, if not exactly autochthonous, term 'partner-ship' by 'partenariato', which sounds more ethnic but which entered the language via the French 'partenariat'. The Portuguese 'partenariado' is evidence of the same impoverishment. Nor can English escape this phe-nomenon: 'speeches' become 'interventions', people 'effectuate actions' rather than 'take steps'; a point is 'tangential' instead of 'irrelevant'; and a 'second-best solution' replaces a 'compromise'.

Because the different language versions of legislative acts are of equal legal value, translators receive instructions to translate legislative texts in an 'amendable' way, which means staying as close to the source text as possible, so that the parts of the text that are amended are easy to trace at the various stages of law-making, and the language units of the text are easy to compare. While the policy is understandable enough in such cases, problems arise when civil service translators apply the same principle to information texts (such as letters and booklets) intended for the general reader; texts of this kind will not work in 'Eurospeak'. As a result, transla-tions often have an after-taste of the original (usually English or French) and a less autochthonous flavour. Freelance translators can help to improve the readability of texts produced by the EU. Together with civil service linguists, freelance translators help to gain acceptance for the European idea and Europe in action; we are jointly responsible for the linguistic quality of documents produced by EU staff. Good communications will help to improve understanding of the very concept of the EU, a concept that has been less than clear for far too long. Indeed, this is one of the factors behind the quality problems that are increasingly appearing in outside translations: for various reasons, the linguistic and drafting quality of original texts is falling off, and freelance translators are finding it increasingly difficult even to decipher them. A concern for the quality of communication has not escaped the attention of Europe's decision-makers. In 1992, both Jacques Delors and the Edinburgh European Council stressed the need for all Community texts to be more readable and hence more accessible to the general public. More recently, the Commission translation service has been campaigning for correct usage and plainer language.

What does the future hold? How will multilingualism and the EU's language policy adjust to the forthcoming rounds of enlargement? What will be the place of the freelance translator in the way language services are organised? How will freelance translators' work develop in future? In the increasingly globalised world of the Internet, freelance translators will be less likely to live in their countries of origin. Perhaps they will work in a country that speaks a variant of their mother tongue, or a country with a different language altogether. In either case, are they not bound to encounter the same problems that are facing civil servants in the European institutions today? Only time will reveal the answers.

## Notes

1. Of course, the institutions' multilingual policy has its practical limits: not all the Member States insisted that their national language should be recognised as an official and / or working language of the Communities. There is also the question of minority languages, which are officially recognised at national level in several Member States.
2. European Parliament Document 1–306/82 (PE 73.706), 21 June 1982.
3. In the case of Dutch, the new edition of the Van Dale monolingual dictionary has included some 8700 new entries, collected over the past ten years. Only 10 % of these words are of English origin.
4. See Roger Goffin, 'Eurolecte: le langage d'une Europe communautaire en devenir'. In Terminologie et Traduction, Office of Official Publications of the EC, Luxembourg 1/1997.
5. But this does not entitle us to write or translate in an opaque and hermetic language, a point we shall return to later.

*Chapter 7*

# Translation and Computerisation at the EU Parliament

ANNE TUCKER

## Introduction

There is no doubt that developments in computer technology since the beginning of the 1980s have had a substantial impact on the work of the translator, as they have had on the work of all those concerned, in one way or another, with processing information. The object of the translation exercise of course remains unchanged: to produce in one language (the target language) a fluent and accurate rendering of a text written in another language (source language). This exercise still requires the same intellectual skills of the translator, but the physical tools and aids he or she uses to perform the task are no longer those of 20 years ago.

In a large international organisation such as the European Parliament, translation is a key activity which is essential to the functioning of the institution as a whole. It also involves a large number of staff: out of a total of some 4500 European Parliament employees, around 950, or 21%, work in the language services (not including interpretation). Of these, about 550 are translators, responsible for translating documents into the 11 official languages of the EU and the rest are secretarial, administrative and support staff. It is clear that an operation on this scale requires not only highly skilled translators but also a large amount of management and coordination. These organisational activities have also changed as a result of the introduction of computers.

This account of the progressive introduction of computer-based technologies in translation relates to the specific example of translation at the European Parliament. The experiences and practices of other large organisations will be different in the details, although the general trends are the same. In smaller organisations and companies the rate of change may be different; some are prevented by financial constraints from make the necessary investment in equipment and software, and lag behind, while others, unrestrained by the sometimes slow-turning wheels of a bureaucracy, are forging ahead.

## Translation Before the Computer

Twenty years ago, translators at the European Parliament, as elsewhere, worked in essentially the same way as translators had always done, using the only writing tools available – pen and paper and the typewriter. They wrote or typed their translations, which were first passed on to a reviser and then to a typing pool where they were retyped, with as many carbon copies as needed, and sent back to the requesting services.

A valuable additional tool, the first contribution of modern technology apart from the electric typewriter, was the dictating machine or 'dictaphone'. It liberated translators with limited or reluctant typing skills and freed their hands and their brains for the non-mechanical tasks of translation – consultation of reference materials and the creative translation process itself. The workload of the typing pools was thereby increased, however, since they generally had to type translations twice: once from the tape dictated by the translator and again after this first version had been corrected by the translator and reviser.

Reference materials were also entirely traditional. For terminological research there was the usual range of dictionaries: bilingual and monolingual, general and specialised. A separate division responsible for terminology provided institution-specific reference material in the form of paper glossaries. To supplement this, individual translators gathered their own terminology store in card index files. For background research and technical material they could turn to a library of encyclopaedias and specialised reference works. All EU-related documentation, including past translations, was stored in large archives housing files of printed documents and carbon copies.

There was no workflow system as such or certainly not with that name. Documents were sent for translation by the requesting services via a system of pneumatic tubes and the completed translations were returned by the same route. Requests were logged in a register on their arrival, the jobs were distributed to translators and each job was logged out when completed and dispatched.

## Rudimentary Office Tools

The first major change to these long-established working arrangements came with the introduction of word-processing terminals in the European Parliament. The first such terminals were delivered in 1982, two for each translation division's typing pool. In the course of the 1980s the number of terminals progressively increased, such that by 1990 all typists in the translation service were using a word processor. During this period also, the equipment and software were renewed and the dedicated word-processing terminals connected to a single server were replaced by fully functional PCs linked in to a local network.

The introduction of word processors did not initially have a great impact on the work of translators, who continued to use the typewriter and the dictaphone, but it did reduce and simplify the work of the typing pool. Secretaries no longer had to retype from scratch the revised versions of translations, and carbon copies became a thing of the past. The setting-up of a local network allowed for the storage and sharing of documents and an electronic document archive began to be built up.

At the same time as the introduction of the first word-processing terminals, an early computer enthusiast in the English translation division, now Director-General of Translation and General Services at the European Parliament and author of the opening section of this book, developed the first version of a production management system, written in the Basic programming language. Also during this period, a few teletype terminals were installed in the translation divisions to give access, albeit via a laborious connection and retrieval procedure, to online databases such as the European Commission's Eurodicautom term base and the CELEX base of EU law.

As previously explained, these initial manifestations of computer technology did not qualitatively affect the job of translation itself. In particular, journeying to a teletype terminal to attempt the long connection process to a remote database was far more time-consuming than consulting paper sources and was undertaken only as a last resort.

## The Desktop Computer

It was not until the arrival of the personal computer (PC) on their own desks that translators began seriously to feel the effects of computer technology on their work. The process of equipping European Parliament translators with computers began in 1990, the first PCs being allocated to only a limited number of translators, those who expressed interest in experimenting with new tools and were not deterred by the relative user-unfriendliness of the MS-DOS operating system. Interest in, and receptivity to, the facilities offered by the PC grew, and by the time of the institution-wide switch to the Windows operating system in 1995–96 all translators were equipped with their own computer. What had begun as an optional tool had now become standard, and its widespread use brought with it widespread changes in the working methods of translators.

First, the PC gave translators the opportunity to use a word processor, previously reserved for secretaries alone. This brought with it both benefits and drawbacks. For those who had previously typed their translations and had good keyboard skills it offered the freedom and flexibility of no longer having to finalise every rendition before committing it to paper: text could be changed, rearranged and deleted quickly and easily. But it also encouraged translators, implicitly at least, to concern themselves with the 'non-translation' aspects of their texts, notably presentation and formatting. Whereas previously they had been able to produce a fairly roughly-typed text, in the knowledge that it would be retyped in proper form by trained secretaries, their text could now be passed electronically to secretaries, who need only correct it and tidy it up. Although perfect formatting was not demanded of translators, the temptation to produce it was great, and it was judged by some at this time that use of a word processor actually reduced translator productivity. Those translators without keyboard skills or with a dislike of computers chose to stay with the dictaphone.

The presence of the PC on the translator's desk gave access not only to the perhaps questionable benefits of the word processor. Each PC was also a terminal from which remote databases could be consulted without the need to leave the office or even the desk. This opened the way for a change in the work and role of the terminology staff. No longer confined to producing paper glossaries, which were inevitably out of date almost as soon as they were published, terminologists were able to store the products of their research in a database which could be continuously updated and expanded, and which was constantly available to all translators. Thanks to database management software, the data could be accessed and retrieved in a straightforward manner without complex login procedures and search commands. A single European Parliament terminology database was created and the production of glossaries rapidly ceased.

With the PCs and a network came also access to file servers and electronic document stores. Past translations and other parliamentary documents could, provided they had been produced electronically, be consulted and retrieved directly from a server, without the need for a visit to the archives to search through paper files. If texts for translation incorporated passages which had already been translated in the past, these passages could simply be copied over into the new translation by copying and pasting. Retyping was no longer necessary.

The circulation and storage of documents in electronic form also required a more sophisticated workflow system. It was not enough simply to track the arrival of documents and their allocation to translators and secretaries, the documents themselves had to be routed and stored. A document exchange server was set up for the transmission of documents to and from the translation divisions and software was written to dispatch the documents to their appropriate storage location.

By this stage computers could undoubtedly facilitate the work of the translator inasmuch as they brought terminological and documentary resources direct to his or her desk and offered a more efficient retrieval system than the perusal of paper files. But the computer tools available were still relatively cumbersome to use, each one involved a different piece of software and there was little or no direct interface between them. If a translator typing in his word-processing application wished to consult a terminology database, for example, he had to launch the relevant database application, perform a search for the desired term and transfer the result back to the word processor, generally by copying and pasting. To benefit from the new online resources the translator had to learn how to use a sometimes bewildering assortment of different tools.

## Translation Technology

The tools so far described were in a sense general-purpose applications that could be called into service to perform some of the tasks associated with translation. The technology behind them took no account of the translation process itself. Before moving on to the next phase in the introduction of computer tools at the European Parliament it is perhaps useful to recall the background to the development of more translation-specific applications.

Until the beginning of the 1990s, translation technology was, to all intents and purposes, confined to the development of machine translation systems. These large and enormously ambitious systems aimed, initially at least, to provide for fully automatic translation of texts with little or no human intervention. They were designed not to assist translators but rather to replace them, and their first developments in the 1950s and 1960s were largely motivated and funded by the US defense community, which was faced during the Cold War with a wealth of intelligence material to digest. Initial hopes were disappointed, the quality of translation was poor and in the 1970s research efforts largely declined.

The 1980s saw a recovery of interest, with developers and users becoming more realistic about what machine translation could and could not do. Commercial systems, still large mainframe applications, were used by an increasingly large number of companies and organisations to provide 'rough' translations. These could either be used as such for information purposes only or passed to translators who would carry out post editing to produce a more comprehensible and acceptable text. This level and type of use continued throughout the 1980s and into the 1990s.

As a result of the increase in the power and memory capacity of the desktop computer in the early 1990s, it also became possible to run simplified versions of these systems on a PC. This development placed them within the reach of a much wider range of users, notably non-linguist professionals and casual users. In recent years, the growth and popularity of the World Wide Web has opened up enormous new potential for machine translation systems. Both PC-based and on-line systems provide an invaluable tool for Web surfers who otherwise have no means of assessing the content of Web pages in languages other than their own.

Aside from automatic machine translation systems, the increase in computing power in the 1990s also permitted the development of far less ambitious and rather more pragmatic translation tools. Rather than attempting to 'understand' and 'translate' a text, translation memory systems, sometimes known as translation workbenches, simply 'memorise' every sentence translated by translators. If the same or a similar sentence comes up for translation again, the system offers the translator the previous translation, highlighting any differences in the original. Such a system has the clear advantage of producing human rather than machine translation – any translation found will have been produced by a translator – and thus of being more acceptable and more useful to the translator.

It should be recognised that the drive for the development of translation memory systems came primarily not so much from traditional translation departments and agencies but from a new source, the software localisation industry. Localisation, the process of adapting the user interface and documentation of computer applications to the culture and language of the target customers, is a booming business. Time is of the essence, since software companies aim for simultaneous release of their products worldwide, and the textual material is enormously repetitive. The same terms and phrases appear time and again in 'help files', user manuals, menus and dialog boxes. Successive releases of the same product will use much of the same textual material, deviating only where features of the product have changed. It is clear therefore that translation memory systems are, in every sense, made for localisation; they ensure consistency both within a product version and from one version to the next and offer substantial savings in time and effort.

Translation memory systems can also be integrated with other tools to provide 'one stop' access to a collection of resources. As well as searching translation memories for previously translated sentences, such systems can look in terminology databases for occurrences of individual terms. If desired, they can also be coupled with fully automatic machine translation systems which will provide a 'fall-back' translation in the event that no previous translation is found in the translation memory. Ancillary tools have been developed to further improve the performance of translation memory systems. Most notable amongst these are alignment programs, which take a text and its translation to produce a ready-made translation memory. This alleviates the problem of the running-in phase of translation memory systems, during which translators are otherwise obliged to begin working with empty translation memories, typing in their translations without getting anything back in return.

Unlike machine translation systems, the performance of which is generally valued more by non-linguists, translation memory systems are designed for translators and intended to be used by translators. The benefits they can bring in terms of time and effort saved are directly dependent on the probability that any given sentence in a text has at some time already been translated. In the case of localisation material, it is clear that this probability is high. But the localisation industry does not have a monopoly on repetitive texts.

## Integrated Translation Tools

In 1993 the translation services of the European Parliament began a limited experiment with translation memory software. The user interface at that time was not particularly congenial: documents could not be processed in their word processor format and had to be converted before and after using the translation memory system. The alignment software used was far from transparent, it required careful tuning to make it function satisfactorily and deterred all but the most determined users. Nonetheless, the tests showed that certain document types had a sufficiently high level of repetitiveness to make the use of such a system worthwhile. They also revealed a potential for gain not only in time but also in accuracy: the system could pick up small changes in successive versions of a text which the human eye sometimes overlooked.

In the years since those initial tests the user-friendliness of the translation memory system employed has improved markedly. The translator uses the system from within his or her familiar word processor, vocabulary retrieved from the terminology database is inserted at the click of a button and translation memories can be searched not only for entire sentences but also for phrases and individual words. Alignment programs are no longer 'black boxes' but provide a versatile interface to allow for interactive tuning and editing of the results of alignment.

There are essentially two classes of documents that are amenable to translation with a translation memory system: repetitive documents and 'evolutive' documents. The class of repetitive documents covers both documents which are repetitive within themselves, containing sentences or phrases which reappear within the same text, and documents which are drawn up at frequent intervals and are based on standard models. A large number of routine administrative documents produced at the European Parliament fall into this category and it was for this class of documents that the translation memory system was first used. Negotiations have taken place between the translation services and the authors of such documents with a view to bringing about greater standardisation of format and content and thereby improving the performance of the translation memory system. One consequence of this has been that some routine documents can now be 'translated' almost entirely by secretaries using the translation memory system, leaving translators free to deal with the more challenging translation tasks.

'Evolutive' documents are defined as those which evolve over time and go through several stages of drafting and translation before a final version is produced. At the European Parliament this class includes the most important documents produced by the institution, the parliamentary reports on proposals for EU legislation. Because of the sensitivity of these documents and the complexity of the drafting and revision procedures involved in their evolution, it was recognised that no attempt should be made to translate them using the translation memory system until the system itself was sufficiently stable and user-friendly, and until appropriate administrative arrangements had been put in place to ensure the necessary coordination and quality control. The feasibility of using the translation memory system for such documents will be assessed in 2000, when a trial will be carried out in the 11 translation divisions on all documents related to a single legislative proposal. This exercise will place far greater demands than hitherto on the translation memory system itself and on the administrative and support staff of the translation services. It will require multiple alignments of documents emanating from the other EU institutions, specifically the Commission and the Council, monitoring of textual alterations introduced by legal and other services, and dealing with the ever-present problem at the European Parliament of documents changing their source language from one version to the next.

In parallel with the introduction of the translation memory system, use of which was initially somewhat tentative, other tools were developed to facilitate the work of the translator and secretary. It has been pointed out earlier that use of a word processor sometimes resulted in a fall in productivity among translators who were tempted to concern themselves over much with text presentation and formatting. This problem was largely solved by the development of a system of word processor macros that could be used by translators and secretaries alike to 'generate' standard document types in the required format. Having launched the macro for the appropriate document type, the translator or secretary has only to type in the textual components when prompted; the correct appearance and positioning of these components is assured by the macro itself.

To provide more ready access to documentary resources, database applications were written for document management and retrieval. These enabled translators to search for previously translated texts according to a wide range of criteria, and to retrieve these texts into their word processor for consultation or further processing. The transmission of documents to and from the translation services was further automated by a workflow system which maps the entire processing circuit of a given document type from inception through to final publication. Under this system, a text released by the authoring service for translation is dispatched electronically to a specific location on file servers in the translation service. Once the translations are completed, the texts are again forwarded automatically to the services responsible for the next stage of processing.

## The Amorphous Document

It has been seen that the computer tools now available to translators relieve them of having to concern themselves with the non-textual components of documents. Translation memory systems operate by processing the source language text of a document, and thereby retain the formatting and structure of the original. Where the translation memory system is not used, macros are available to format translated texts. The question that now arises is whether translators need even to be aware of the formatting of a text.

Before the arrival of the computer, the status of a document was clear. Authoring services produced a typed text, formatted as they wished it to appear when printed. The translation services produced a typed translation of the text, also formatted ready for printing. The document was the typed text. Now, however, a single text can give rise to different documents in different forms. A translated text may be converted to one format for electronic printing, another format for publication on the Internet, and yet another format for storage in a document repository. It is, moreover, quite possible that none of these formats will be the word processor format used within the translation services. The text of a document can thus be divorced from the structure of the document.

The word processor macro system described earlier has already been expanded so as to incorporate structural markers in the documents it generates. These are designed to facilitate the conversion of documents to other formats and to permit the extraction of certain elements, such as dates and titles, for indexing purposes. The next logical step in this process is to abstract completely all structural information from the documents sent for translation. At the time a document is first created by an authoring service, its structure can be generated independently by a purpose-built application. The text of the document is subsequently inserted into this structure. The structural information travels with the document during the subsequent stages of its processing, including translation, but this information need not be made visible. All that matters is that the software applications used to process the document, such as the translation memory system and the word processor in the case of translation, are not permitted to remove or change this structure. When required, the structural information can be used to generate a version of the document in an appropriate format: word processor format for a translator's draft, HTML for Internet publication, SGML/XML for electronic publishing, etc.

A number of applications applying these principles are now being developed and tested at the European Parliament. Their use places the burden of responsibility on the authoring services for defining and adhering to the appropriate document structure. Invariant textual components, such as generic headings, and variable items that can be retrieved from databases, such as titles, are automatically 'translated' before the texts are sent to the translation services. What is left for translators is the translation of text pure and simple.

## A Single Interface for Reference Material

The setting up of an institutional Intranet at the European Parliament has brought with it the prospect that translators, and indeed other staff, will be able to access all available terminological and documentary resources via a single interface, the Web browser. Through the Intranet, translators are already able to retrieve and consult the full range of the European Parliament's public and internal documentation, from legislative reports to minutes and agendas. Links to the Intranets of other EU institutions give access to their publications also: Official Journals from the Official Publications Office, legislative proposals from the Commission, etc. The terminology databases of the European Parliament and the other EU institutions can now also be consulted via the Intranet, and each has a Web browser interface to facilitate research.

Full access to the World Wide Web has of course opened up all the translation and documentary resources of the outside world, with all the benefits and frustrations that this implies. Whatever the obstacles, however, there is no doubt that the Web offers the most efficient and speedy route for retrieving, say, the text of a UN resolution from UN headquarters in New York. In terms of immediacy and coverage of information, the Web surpasses all the resources previously available.

The success of the World Wide Web has, in a large measure, determined the shape of other computer applications for translators and non-linguists alike. Since the Web browser provides the interface to all resources on the Intranet and Internet, it can also be used as the interface to other, internal, applications, including those of the translation services. Thus the latest versions of the applications in use in the translation services – including the production management and document management programs – are being designed to make use of the same Web browser. There is every reason to expect that in the relatively near future the Web browser will provide the single route to all sources of information for translators, whether documentary, terminological or administrative.

## Dictation

Since the arrival or, as some might still stay, imposition of the PC as the working tool of the translator, successive software developments have aimed at making computer applications easier and less time-consuming to use. At the outset there was a diverse collection of disparate applications, each requiring knowledge of different manipulations and procedures. Gradually this has been honed down to a basic suite of tools: the word processor supplemented by direct links to translation memories and term bases, together with a single interface to other reference materials.

However, the developments so far described do not offer a solution to those translators who are still not at ease working with a keyboard and who know that they are more productive dictating their translations to a dictaphone or directly to a typist. There are still many who, while they may use their computers for consulting reference material, do not resort to the word processor for producing their translations. It is with a view to meeting their needs that the European Parliament's translation services are now starting to introduce voice recognition software.

Until relatively recently, voice recognition programs did not offer the versatility and flexibility required for the dictation of texts covering all possible ranges of subject matter in a variety of working conditions. They required a substantial period of familiarisation with the voice of each individual user, worked best when the subject matter was confined to a specific area such as the medical field and, most restrictively, demanded that the user enunciate each word separately, in discrete rather than continuous speech.

Technology has since advanced, however, and the latest versions of the products available on the market show far greater potential. Continuous speech can now be recognised, the subject matter need not be constrained, and the familiarisation stage, although still recommended, is much shorter. At the current rate of progress, it seems reasonable to assume that such systems will, in the near future, be able to perform with almost the accuracy, and certainly the speed, of a typist taking dictation.

For the European Parliament's translation services, the conditions which have determined if and when voice recognition systems can be introduced as standard tools have been twofold: first, their integration with the software tools currently in use; and, second, their ability to deal with all 11 EU official languages. As far as the first condition is concerned, integration with both the word processor and the translation memory system is now assured. The second condition is proving more difficult to meet since it is determined by commercial factors. While there is sufficient demand to justify the research and investment involved in developing voice recognition systems for the more widely-used European languages, the potential market for, say, Greek or Danish, is much smaller and it may be some time yet before such systems are commercially available. As a result, the software available can be used only in the English, French, German, Spanish, Italian and Dutch translation divisions and its use cannot, therefore, be made standard.

## Machine Translation

Discussion of the use of machine translation has been left until late in this account, because machine translation is largely incidental to the work of the translation services at the European Parliament and is likely to remain so for the foreseeable future. As explained earlier, machine translation is a valuable tool for non-linguists who wish to ascertain the content of a text written in a language of which they have no knowledge, but it does not provide a publication-ready text in the target language. Staff and Members of the European Parliament have remote access to the Systran machine translation system of the Commission of the EU: they can email documents to the Systran service which sends back the translations by return mail.

This service is used occasionally by parliamentary bodies which have insufficient time or insufficient resources to send their documents to the translation services, or which require translations for information purposes only. Use in the translation services themselves is very limited and confined to those language combinations in which machine translation performs reasonably well, namely those with a more-or-less parallel sentence structure. Thus a machine translation of a French text may provide useful starting material for a Spanish translator, but is of little or no use to a German translator.

In contrast, however, it must be recognised that machine translation is widely used and valued at the Commission of the European Union, including in its translation services. To explain this difference in receptivity, it is important to recognise the difference in the work and roles of the two institutions. The Commission, as the executive body, has to digest an enormous amount of technical or specialist material, which may or may not be directly relevant to the matter at issue. A large amount of this documentation is processed for internal use only and it is here that machine translation offers valuable assistance and considerable time saving. If required, a post-editing service is provided by the translation services to turn the raw output of the machine translation into a more readable target language text.

The European Parliament, however, is the democratically accountable institution representing the citizens of Europe. As a political body it is concerned to ensure that all its work and activities are made known to the general public. The documents processed by the translation services, such as the proceedings of Parliament and its committees, their reports and opinions, and the policy documents of the political groups, are, with very few exceptions, intended for general publication. In these circumstances the 'rough' translation quality supplied by machine translation is unacceptable. Since the European citizen is already critical of the sometimes unavoidable use of 'Eurospeak' in EU documentation, he or she is unlikely to take kindly to the vagaries of machine translation.

## Freelance Translation and Home Working

As this account is based on first-hand experience of work within a large translation service, it has not paid specific attention to the case of the freelance translator working alone. It goes without saying, however, that the introduction of computer-based translation tools has had an impact on the freelance worker, even if he or she is not directly concerned with developments in workflow and document management systems. The European Parliament currently entrusts some 10 % of its translation work to freelance translators and this percentage is set to rise to 20 % in the near future.

It is now generally accepted that freelance translators should be able to receive their source texts electronically, by email, should produce their translations with a word processor and should return them to their clients electronically. Increasingly they are also being asked to make use of translation workbench systems, using translation memories supplied by their clients. The World Wide Web has also given freelance translators the same access as in-house translators to public terminology databases and documentary resources.

This naturally prompts the question as to why, in increasingly budget-conscious organisations, staff translators should be required to travel to work, and occupy costly office space, if they can carry out their duties with access to the same resources, and at their own better convenience, from home. In 1996 the European Parliament's translation service began a pilot trial of home-working, involving some 20 translators who had expressed the wish to work from home. These translators were equipped by the institution with computers and modems, and received and returned their work via the electronic mail system.

It is not, however, strictly true to say that these home-workers had access to the same resources as in-house translators. Because they were not connected to the European Parliament's internal computer network and file servers they could not retrieve directly any internal documents which might be of relevance to their translation and had to request such documents be sent by email. Nor did they have direct access to internal terminology databases and translation memories; they had to get by instead with copies of these databases installed on their own PCs, with the inevitable consequence that the information contained in them could not be kept up to date. The home-workers were therefore in essentially the same position as freelance translators; they could make use of all publicly available resources but not those to which only staff translators working in their offices had access.

As a result of further advances in telecommunications technology, this situation has also changed. It is now possible to link the computers of home-workers into the European Parliament's internal network while at the same time guaranteeing the necessary security to protect this network from unauthorised external access. Home-workers now share the same computer configuration as in-house staff and have access to all the same facilities. Email communication is no longer necessary for the exchange of translation work and documentation. The home-worker's office has, in effect, become an extension of the European Parliament's premises. The only remaining, and currently insurmountable, disadvantage suffered by the home-worker is the fact that he or she cannot take a short stroll to consult, or have a coffee with, the colleague in the office next door.

## Conclusions

It should be clear from this account that, while the impact of the computer on translation has been considerable, it has in no sense called into question the central role of the translator, whose skills remain as essential as ever. Fears that computerised translation tools might somehow replace the human translator have been shown to be completely unfounded, and will remain so.

What the computer has done, in essence, is to relieve translators of clerical and repetitive work not directly related to the process of translation, to facilitate their research work, and to enable them to concentrate their time on the job in hand. It would, of course, be naïve to imagine that computer tools have been introduced in the European Parliament, or in any other organisation, for the sole purpose of making life easier for translators. The managerial motivation is rationalisation and increased productivity, which in translation terms means more pages for fewer staff.

Centralised management of a single terminology database has already reduced the number of staff employed in terminology research and eliminated the reduplication of effort involved in maintaining multiple individual terminology collections. The use of word processors and voice recognition systems by translators will ultimately remove entirely the need for typing staff, although some secretaries can well be redeployed in ancillary translation tasks such as aligning texts to supplement translation memories and creating 'pre-translations' using a translation workbench. Automatic electronic storage of all documentary resources will enable translation departments to dispense with archivists and document distribution services, and automated workflow systems will reduce the need for clerical staff to process translation requests.

And what of the translators themselves? The EU currently has 11 official languages, which means that translators are required to work from and into a total of 110 different language pairs. In the years ahead, with the accession of the Central and Eastern European countries, the number of official languages could to rise to 22, giving a total of 462 different language pairs. In these circumstances it is clear that some form of rationalisation, or rather reorganisation, will be necessary to avoid an exponential increase in the size of the translation services of the EU institutions which is neither logistically nor financially tenable. Computerised translation tools will help to increase the productivity of the individual translator, they will allow him or her the flexibility and mobility to perhaps solve the problem of inadequate office space, but they will not of themselves answer the question of how to arrange most economically for the translation of documents from each of 22 languages into 21 others. This is the challenge now facing the institutions of the EU and a separate article will have to be written on how they rise to this challenge.

## Chapter 8

# Translating Transparency in the EU Commission

LUCA TOMASI

As we prepare to enter a knowledge-based, globalised society, translators are bound to occupy a central position as the specialised brokers of valuable goods. It may therefore be interesting to examine, in the light of the ongoing technological, social and political changes, how that huge stock exchange of languages, the Translation Service of the European Commission, is equipping itself to answer the challenges of the 21st century.

Discussing the effects of the introduction of writing, Walter J. Ong (1982: 81) comments that 'intelligence is relentlessly reflexive, so that even the external tools that it uses to implement its workings become "internalised", that is, part of its own reflective process'. The human mind, apparently, gradually became accustomed to processes like writing and printing, so that it now considers them 'natural', while it still regards new technologies such as the computer as 'artificial'; as a matter of fact, Ong argues, 'There is no way to write "naturally".' The computer revolution, therefore, will only be a secondary or tertiary innovation, far less drastic in its effects than the spread of the alphabet or the invention of the printing press. It is, nevertheless, an important breakthrough and its impact on our use of language and on our thought structures will be far-reaching.

What, then, are the most visible consequences of the advent of personal computers (PCs) on our desks, as well as in our homes and in many workplaces, from manufacturing industries to banks and travel agencies? I will not analyse here in detail the successive steps of 'modernisation' at the Commission Translation service, as they largely parallel those at the European Parliament, already covered in Anne Tucker's contribution to the present volume; I would prefer to examine how the electronic age is influencing our approach to translation in the institutions of the EU.

## From Handwriting to the Hypertext

Several powerful forces are acting simultaneously on our languages, modifying their internal dynamics and their reciprocal relationships. Globalisation, with its unprecedented acceleration of world trade and cultural exchanges, is merely the most recent one as well as being a trendy byword; however, an equally important shift was initiated in the first decades of the 20th century. With the progressive spread of the telephone, radio and various forms of sound recording, our society entered a new, or secondary orality, which bears striking similarities to the old one, but with remarkable differences. It is similar in that it fosters a sense of belonging to a group and a concentration on the present moment, on instantness – but it is self-consciously oral, based as it is on the use of writing and print.

The telegraph and telex machine, with their coding and sequential processing of the word, seemed to go in the opposite direction, and facsimiles and e-mail offered, for the first time, the opportunity of reducing to a handful of seconds the delay between the writing and reading of a written communication. The motion pictures, originally voiceless, were first accompanied by live music and then by actual dialogue, and television completed the integration between image and sound, while maintaining a strong emphasis on the visual and spatial aspects.

The GSM phone followed the inverse path: created to ensure instantaneous oral contact, anywhere, anytime, it almost immediately developed into a hybrid instrument, capable of sending and receiving SMS (the acronym for 'short message services', including text and a few pre-defined 'icons'), and the latest models are now sold with a larger display for browsing the Internet and an alphabetic keyboard for easier typing. Finally, the Internet introduced an added element of interactive multimediality: even if the visual elements (text and images) still prevail, it increasingly includes sound files and connections to sites offering music, news and real-time hard-core groans and sighs.

What is more important for our purpose, however, is that with the arrival of the HyperText Markup Language and its successors, the traditional sequentiality of written text has been broken. Web pages are not ordered units to be read in succession, line by line, one after the other, but rather neurones linked by mysterious synapses to other, often unpredictable terminals. We rarely take the time to read them through or even to move past the initial screen, before surfing away to some other page.

What has this rather pedantic exposition to do with work at the Translation Service of the European Commission? The fact is that we are not only using all these instruments in our daily life to keep us up to date or to facilitate our work, we are also heavily influenced by these tools, interiorising them as we have interiorised writing in the last 2000 years and printing since the 16th century.

The conflicting forces behind these instruments radically modify our approach to the outside world and, to a greater extent, to our everyday job as translators. They are not, of course, the only influences acting on the European language landscape. Political events such as the unification of Germany, past and future enlargements, immigration and regional requests for linguistic autonomy have put our present 11 languages under heavy pressure; but the subtle action of technological development on language is often less recognised and deserves adequate study.

What I am suggesting is that we are living in an environment in which a translation, or at least an acceptable equivalent in another language, can often be obtained at the click of a mouse. Even better, the most recent versions of popular browsers are able to tell what your linguistic preferences are and to choose the right page to show you.

## Translation On-line

Several search engines and software companies offer instant translations of text and web pages. The results, however, are often discouraging. This is a paragraph taken from the European Parliament pages and translated into French by InterTran[1] software:

### 3. The key players

At Union level, respect for human rights is a matter which concerns, on the one hand, each of the Community institutions and, on the other, each Member State individually. Of the institutions, Parliament and the Court of Justice play a particularly important role in devising and implementing the EU's human rights policy.

### 3. Les touche musicienne

À Union égaliser, respecter pour être humain équitable c'est une substance quoi toucher, one les une écriture, chaque de les Communauté institutions et, one les autre, chaque Membre État individuellement. De les institutions, Parlement et les Tribunal de Justice pièce de théâtre une particulièrement important rôle dans [devising] et ustensile les [EU's] être humain équitable politique.

This is the same paragraph translated from French into English:

### 3. Les acteurs

Au niveau de l'Union, le respect des droits de l'homme concerne d'un côté chacune des institutions et de l'autre chaque Etat membre individuellement. Parmi les institutions communautaires, le Parlement européen et la Cour de justice ont un rôle particulièrement important dans la conception et la concrétisation de la politique de l'UE relative aux droits de l'homme.

### 3. The cast

At the level about [l'Union], him abidance any dues about the man [concerne] [d'un] side each any institutions and about [l'autre] any [Etat] fellow individually. Amid the institutions communal, him Parliament Europe and her Court about equity drove a involvement especially important at her conception and her [concrétisation] any political about [l'UE] comparative at the dues about the man.

It is true that this software offers, for each word, many alternative translations, but the dictionary itself is very limited. The first two options for the common Internet term 'Interesting links', for instance, are 'Intéressant terrain de golf' and 'Intéressant liaisons'. Better results can be obtained with *Systran Translation software*,[2] offered on a popular search engine:

### 3. Les joueurs principaux

Au niveau des syndicats, le respect pour des droits de l'homme est une question qui concerne, d'une part, chacun des établissements de la Communauté et, de l'autre, de chaque Etat membre individuellement. Des établissements, le Parlement et la Cour de Justice jouent un rôle particulièrement important en concevant et en mettant en application la politique de droits de l'homme d'EU's.

Excessive confidence in the capabilities of translation software produces at times involuntarily comical results. The Forensic Science Division of the Michigan State Police, for instance, offers its website in English, French, Italian and Spanish. The three latter versions were translated on-line by Systran Translation software – and show no trace of editing. The Mission statement runs like this: 'La division légale de la science fournira la conduite, le développement, la coordination et la livraison des services légaux « du dernier cri » à la communauté criminelle de justice'. In addition, it is stated that 'Les membres de notre «peloton de bombe» sont les dispositits explosifs improvisés 'rendre-sûrs' invités et occasionnellement unexploded l'ordonnance militaire.'

Apart from this undiscriminating reliance on technological tools, however, commercial companies, public institutions and individuals are increasingly aware of the need for multilingual presentations to exploit fully the potentialities of the World Wide Web.

At the same time, the traditional distinction between the written and spoken word is becoming increasingly blurred. The very fact that the spoken contributions to a seminar which make up the bulk of this volume are written down would seem to attest to the enduring primacy of the written word: the speeches of the participants to the workshop are written down, committed to paper in order to give them a wider 'audience' and longer life. But again, things are not so clear-cut. Many of these contributions were probably written down and polished *before* being delivered to a 'live' public of hearers, and some of them might have been recorded on tape and written down afterwards. In addition, they might end up on the Internet, where they could be read aloud by some vocal synthesiser to a blind person, maybe after automatic translation in some other language.

Voice recognition software is also progressing rapidly, and is being developed in a growing number of languages. As accuracy increases and prices go down, it can be foreseen that in a few years it will be part and parcel of standard application packages. Once the microphone is accepted as a supplementary input device along with the keyboard, the voice and the hands will equally contribute to delivering the message – thus realising, it has been malignantly observed, the dream of Italian translators.

## The Resurrection of the Word

The forces which are shaping our present and future society affect our work environment, putting at our disposal tools which were hardly imaginable only a decade ago, while they profoundly modify the attitudes and expectations of our 'clients', that is the services where the originals we translate are drafted and, more importantly, of the public at large. If transparency and accountability are to be more than empty catchwords, the public has a right to expect a timely and understandable translation not only of legislative acts already adopted, but also of any important paper produced or discussed within our institutions. White and green books, contributions to the EU summits, proposals for decisions, directives and regulations must all be available on the net for everybody to read, judge and react to.

Hyperlinks must also be provided for jumping from one language version to another, from one piece of legislation to the legal basis in the treaties or to the implementation measures adopted by the Member States. This, of course, is not the job of translators, but rather of a new brand of assistants, responsible for the electronic layout of the translated documents. As the vertical integration of tasks proceeds, bringing keyboard input and terminological research increasingly into the job description of the standard translator, typing pools will increasingly take up other functions. One of these could be ensuring that every document fed to the web is adequately linked to the relevant pages. Translators, however, will have to develop a consciousness of this aspect, as it will influence the quality of the texts on which they are working.

It is not easy to assess the full extent and direction of such changes, and we can only guess where they will take us. Electronic texts have already familiarised us in recent years with a new kind of instability. One of the traditional attributes of the written word, further intensified by print, was of course its permanence, its definitive nature. Poets and writers have often – and paradoxically – equated writing to death, as opposed to the living spoken word. Plato's Socrates was of course the first critic of writing, but also one of the best examples of the power of the alphabet and, as has been noted, a product of the revolution of thought made possible by writing. The spoken language is the spirit, the *pneuma*, whereas the letter – the marks left on a stone, a clay tablet or a sheet of paper – inevitably tends to hypostatise the concept.

Now electronic processing of the word has again changed our paradigm: the original texts coming in for translation from the various Commission services show a disturbing tendency to shift, to change all the time. Multiple versions of the same document, which until recently were an inevitable feature of politically controversial papers, are nowadays commonplace, as a consequence of the use of word-processing in the Directorates General. One might argue that the texts to be translated in the past had undergone more careful thought, as our colleagues were aware of the lengthy process of retyping entire sections. Or it may be that the quality of today's documents has improved, as the author services have an added opportunity for clarifying their meaning until the very last minute, including in response to the comments and suggestions of puzzled translators. The result, however, is that we find ourselves working on more amorphous material, which has prompted the use of a whole range of new tools to track changes, additions and replacements.

## Repetita Iuvant

Let us take a concrete example: the 'Agenda 2000' set of documents, with the regular Commission reports on the preparation of candidate countries for accession to the EU. Every year, the responsible Commission services prepare a bulky document for each candidate state, analysing chapter by chapter its progress in the adoption of the Community *acquis*,[3] the results of the screening exercise, its response to the Copenhagen political and economic criteria etc. Focusing on the advances made in comparison to the preceding year, these documents have to be produced, or at least modified, at the 11th hour. One of their main features is repetitiveness. First of all internal repetitiveness, as the formulas used in commenting on the state of things ('The current staff of the Ministry is XXX') or last year's developments ('Although positive results have been achieved, further progress is needed . . . ') only allow for limited variants. Second, the authors of the various contributions that go into the global document tend to base theirs on the paper prepared for the previous year, which involves, so to speak, a 'historical' repetitiveness. Finally, as the structure of the documents and the recent history of the countries in question are often the same, there is a 'parallel' similarity amongst the reports relating to these countries.

The Translation Service of the European Commission, which is called upon to translate thousands of pages in the shortest possible time, is thus confronted with an opportunity–repetitions mean that large chunks of text need not be translated anew each time – and a challenge – consistency. It is true that we have plenty of material to help us translate this vast mass of writing and powerful instruments to search for the right phrase. Indeed, the wealth of our databases is almost daunting: a search on our Intranet with 'Agenda 2000' as a keyword will produce almost 6000 documents.

The problem is therefore how to best coordinate our efforts in order to produce a timely, accurate and consistent translation of the reports. Several translators will, of course, have to participate in this effort, which often implies working late at night or over the weekend. The electronic tools at their disposal include the so-called translator's workbenches, stored memories of previously translated similar texts, access to all reference documents and databases, the Internet, online dictionaries on CD-ROM, etc. On the negative side, the subjects are extremely varied, covering the entire _acquis_ and a trade-off has to be made between internal consistency and the specialisation of the translators involved. Moreover, the latter do not receive the 'final' versions until very late in the process, and have to work on sections as they become available. The usefulness of computer resources, also, is at times limited by the unfortunate fact that the language of the original can change: while version one of a section was written in French, you may receive a fresh revision in English, making your French to Italian translation memory worthless.

Team spirit, flexibility and a good command of all the available instruments seem to be the main qualities required of translators in such an exercise. Good support, in terms of electronic libraries, searchable files and administration of the inflow and outflow of documents, is also fundamental. Quite apart from very hard feelings towards those in charge of the original documents, furthermore, whoever participates in this effort is

inevitably bound to develop a new way of perceiving the words themselves and his or her world. There is nothing static, nothing definitive in the
millions of words coming and going along the telephone lines of the Translation Service between September and November. Everything can and
does change overnight, and the number of pages translated is a multiple of
the final output. At the same time, there is a growing consciousness that the
translation will not end up in some dusty shelf of a far off library, but rather
will be immediately put into the cyberspace, for all interested parties to see,
and will feed a memory for years to come.

The electronic word therefore discovers new life, one utterly unknown
to printed texts. Such a vitality is not always a blessing to translators, contributing to the Protean quality of the originals and exposing them, through
increased visibility, to the constant judgement of the press and public
opinion. However, it can have a central role in their motivation and add an
element of challenge to their day-to-day jobs. After all, producing legislation and other documents is one of the key tasks of the European
Commission.

Given such an environment, there is a very strong case for working out a
more explicit language policy at the Commission's Translation Service.
While retaining many of its original and fascinating features, our work has
evolved from the state of a craft to that of a modern profession, involving
groupwork and life-long learning. Demonstrating good translation skills
in a competition is not enough to be able to participate in such large projects
as the Research and Development Framework Programme or the annual
General Budget exercise. Language policy cannot be left to the choices of
individual translators, nor should it be driven by what is new on the
software market. A deliberate effort must be made to develop a formal
language policy for the Service, covering recommended guidelines for
such diverse and sensible issues as layout and the use of foreign words,
clarity and the relationships with national legislation. Unless we are able to
produce first class work, all plead about the transparency of the European
institutions will be meaningless.

## The Problem of Quality

Consistency is not the only aspect requiring attention as the number of
translators increases; more importantly, there is the problem of quality. It is
not uncommon for Directorates General with tight deadlines to circulate
texts produced by machine-translation software, after a perfunctory
editing. Furthermore, the very power of the tools at our disposal, combined
with heavy workloads, involves the risk of overestimating their capabilities. Unlike total output and meeting assigned deadlines, quality is difficult

to assess and it is not always duly rewarded by the existing evaluation and promotion schemes.

An additional problem lies in the very concept behind the new applications in use for computer-assisted translation. The exciting developments of information technology, with soaring increases in the volumes of memory and speed of processing, have prompted a different approach. Back in the 1950s, conscious of the limits of computing capacity, theoreticians and pioneers of machine translation envisaged a 'semantic' approach, whereby a computer program actually tried to interpret a sentence or a phrase in a language, analysing its components, to produce its equivalent in another language.

This still is, very roughly, the basic philosophy of machine-translation services found on the Internet. They have gained in speed but the approach is largely the same: to create a new sentence, the program must find the verb, noun and various parts of speech, so that it can fetch their linguistic counterparts and place everything in its proper place. The system further developed at the European Commission can also be adapted through profiles and special glossaries to improve accuracy. There has been some progress, and a significant number of pages is daily processed in this way for subsequent post-editing by human translators, but all in all this path has proven disappointing. To improve the accuracy of results, segments of translated texts are constantly validated by the machine-translation staff and memorised into the system.

The most recent aids to translation have been developed in the light of new technological advances and therefore make use of much larger memory repositories and processing power to implement a statistical or probabilistic approach. The recognition of written or vocal input is based on similarities to previously memorised sentences or on a language model with a description of its most common word sequences. To assess the probability of finding a word in a given place, speech recognition systems – as well as optical character recognition applications used to scan a printed page and transform it in electronic text format – typically make use of *trigrams* or combinations of three words. The strength of this method is its simplicity: to establish the algorithms of a language model, it is sufficient to feed large volumes of data into a computer, which creates the probability tables. This, however, does not take into account long-range grammatical dependencies and additional rules have to be given to the software in order to make it more efficient.

Moving from very different starting points, then, the two philosophies seem now to be converging: a combination of powerful algorithms of probabilistic distribution and grammatical interpretation holds the hope of more powerful tools to assist the translators.

Our offices have undergone significant change in recent years; more changes are to be expected in the years to come. Already, it is now not uncommon to see people sitting back in their chairs in front of multi-coloured computer screens. The main window on the computer screen displays the pre-processed text, with different colours and shadings to highlight changes in the original, total or partial match with previously translated segments, or machine translation. Smaller windows show the similar or identical segments existing in the translation memory and the results of automatic consultation of a terminology database. The software can automatically recognise and substitute dates and numbers. All that remains for the translator to do is to dictate amendments to the sentences proposed one by one by the computer screen or to browse in the many data-bases, dictionaries and search engines locally or remotely available on the Internet.

These new working methods, however, also imply a different attitude on the part of the translators, especially in the editing or reviewing phase. As a matter of fact, mistakes made by this kind of software are extremely difficult to spot. Spellcheckers are powerless against such blunders as *'un nonno europeo'* for *'Unione europea'* ('a European grandfather' instead of 'European Union') and grammar checkers are still too young to provide real help. Constant attention is required to ensure that the output actually corresponds to the best quality standards.

Statistical analysis is of tremendous help, and it will certainly go a long way towards ensuring the consistency of lexical and syntactical choices across the board in our Service; it could even prove useful to a certain standardisation of language in accordance with 'European' usage derived from glossaries and databases. At the same time, the mechanical and repetitive character of computer-assisted translation involves the very real risk of passively accepting whatever the computer proposes. And this risk is now magnified by the technological drive: every time that we tolerate linguistic sloppiness on the part of some computer program (or 'entropy', as the technicians call it), we validate that choice and it will be suggested the next time the same or a similar sentence comes up in an original.

## Conclusion

The global impact of technological change on our attitudes towards language is twofold.

On the one hand, the printed or electronic word of the original texts produced by other services has lost most of its steadiness and appears more and more volatile. This is very annoying: how can you be expected to take seriously a document which you already know will be revised several times, scrapping or rewriting those very paragraphs on which you are bound to focus your best efforts?

On the other hand, we are developing a growing consciousness of the permanence and visibility of our translations. In spite of our state-of-the-art equipment, they are the Rosetta stones of the EU and the Union's legislation and publications are becoming more and more relevant to the everyday lives of a growing number of European citizens.

As the Commission white and green papers metamorphose into white and green websites and discussion fora, as trade and industry, education, research and all sorts of other activities are integrated, the readership of our translations is rapidly changing. From a restricted circle of experts in European affairs, it is widening to include ordinary citizens, who know nothing about our Community jargon, but still want or need to know what is going on.

To secure their active support, the Union will have to offer them concrete political solutions for their problems and real opportunities for growth. But sound policies and concrete solutions are worthless unless they are formulated clearly, in a language understandable to every European citizen. The need for a realistic and coherent language policy for drafting and translating all documents intended for the general public has never been greater in the European institutions.

## Notes
1. See http://www.tranexp.com:2000/InterTran
2. See http://world.altavista.com/
3. The entire body of European laws is known as Acquis Communautaire.

## References
Ong, Walter J. (1982) *Orality and Literacy – The Technologizing of the Word.* London and New York: Methuen.

## Chapter 9

# Helping the Journalist to Translate for the Reader

CHRISTOPHER COOK

I was fortunate enough to begin my career as a broadcast journalist with a pioneer. For two years I worked with one of that handful of men – and, alas, they were mostly men 50 years ago – who helped to invent British photo-journalism. When *Picture Post*, which was the name of the magazine that they worked for 'closed' a good many moved onto television, to the BBC, where their particular gift for blending words and pictures was admired by audiences and executives alike.

I learnt much from this man, although much of it I have long since for-gotten. However, one thing has stayed with me through 30 years of working as a journalist in television, radio and in print. When that pioneer and I would meet to talk about whatever story it was that we were working on he would always use this phrase about 'the empty chair'. At first I was baffled, but then he explained. If you were broadcasting from a television or a radio studio you had to remember that the empty chair – and it literally could be an empty chair – wasn't really empty at all. It belonged to the audience. In other words the second commandment of journalism (the first having to do with truth and accuracy) was that whether you were broad-casting or writing for a newspaper or a magazine what you were saying or writing was worth next to nothing if no one heard or read you.

Set beside the self-inflated claims that today's global media conglomer-ates make about their communication skills, about reaching the right audiences with the right message at the right time that 'empty chair' sounds a bit home-spun as advice for young journalists or, for that matter, professional translators young and old. Indeed isn't it downright old-fash-ioned in a world of journalism ruled by demographics, IT and commercial synergies all with the single aim of turning news into profits? But if it is an echo from an older world of journalistic practice it is still a lesson that we would do well to attend to, whether we are making the news, translating the news or writing the news. For this phrase 'the empty chair' represents not so much a way of working as the proper cast of mind that all of us whose business it is to communicate need to cultivate. We have a responsibility to engage the reader's or the listener's attention, to speak and write to them as if what was being broadcast or was in print was for their eyes and ears only. There is a natural intimacy about the very best journalism in which simple humanity transcends the technological arsenal that plays an ever-greater part in posting messages to the viewer, listener or reader.

Elsewhere Arturo Tosi has written about the importance of 'transparent communication'. That is a more formal way of saying much the same thing. The best communication, be it journalism or translation, is about reaching an audience and reaching out too beyond the circumstances which may have provoked a particular story or a translation. To modify McLuhan's celebrated dictum from the 1960s the medium isn't the message, but rather it is the message that is the medium.

No one who has observed translators at work within the EU or elsewhere can ever underestimate the difficulties of rendering a growing number of European languages into each other. Naturally the complicated logistics of these operations take your breath away, particularly when one contemplates a future that will almost certainly see an enlarged Union. Equally one cannot but be impressed by the dedication that so many professional interpreters and translators bring to their work. Of no European political institution is this truer than the European Parliament. And it is here I would like to suggest that translators in particular play a pivotal role in making this Parliament work.

There is a sense in which the translator is the Parliament's doorkeeper as he or she expresses in a variety of languages the business that the parliament has done, is about to do and intends to do in a series of written documents. I imagine that a great many of these documents are internal papers with a circulation that is restricted to Members of the Parliament and the administrative officers who ensure its smooth working. And in this case the 'meaning' of what is said may be thought to matter more than the way in which that meaning is expressed. (I appreciate that this is a distinction that many language theorists would refute, but for purely practical purposes that have mostly to do with the way in which lay linguists think about language maybe we can leave such refutations inside the universities.)

What this perhaps means is that while parliamentarians and their officials know exactly what a particular report or memorandum or set of minutes or a paper is about, anyone who is outside the parliamentary circle may well have difficulties in grasping what is at issue. The language used in translation is 'owned' by that small circle and is all but impenetrable to an outsider. But surely it is essential that many of these documents should be fully understood by all of us who are citizens of the member countries of the EU and who elect directly MEPs? We need to know what is being done, so to speak, in our name in Luxembourg and Strasbourg. If we do not understand then the door that translators keep between the citizens of Europe and the business of their Parliament is either permanently closed or, worse, it was never intended that it should be opened. Much graver, in a way, is a scenario in which that door is held ajar and we can just about peer around it to see what is happening beyond, but because of the infelicitous nature of translations we see everything, to mix metaphors, through a glass darkly. Then we develop a dangerously distorted view of the parliament's business that does a disservice to the democratic principle that the new Europe preaches with such conviction.

The news from Europe is mediated for the vast majority of Europeans by journalists. And if journalists are confused about precisely what is happening because of an ill-considered translation that ignores my 'empty chair' principle then they will either cling for dear life to 'gossip' and 'rumour' as the basis of their reporting, or be tempted to take the European parliament less seriously than it deserves. This particularly applies to official reports etc. that, unlike internal parliamentary papers, are deliberately designed for wider public circulation. In this category I would also include press releases. And it is here that we arrive at another truth, or maybe truism about the relationship between journalists and the work of translators.

Good journalists are not idle, but they are busy; and increasingly their editors require them to produce well-informed expert views on a range of complex issues about which they have too little time to prepare themselves. Thus they rely on the information that is provided for them in press releases and associated briefing notes. However, press releases and briefing notes are never neutral; they are designed to make the best possible case for whatever decision has been taken. Thus skilful press releases are invariably written in a style that suits the readership for which they are intended, and if they are well done the grateful journalist, particularly if the subject matter is beyond his or her level of expert comprehension, will simply reshape that release into a report. (The process is perhaps not quite so mechanical as this suggests; nevertheless as a generalised way of describing what can happen it does hold true.) It thus behoves translators to 'help' the media by reproducing this kind of material in other languages in a style that journalists will find sympathetic. However, lest I have given a wrong impression I ought to stress the point that I do not regard it as any part of the translator's task to help to 'spin' the content of a particular document.

For their part I suspect that translators having worked long and hard on a particular document that has then been circulated to the media imagine that their translation is carefully filed in a research library. Or better still it is easily accessed in its original form through the Internet. And when the assiduous journalist needs to he or she will revisit this translated document. But as I have suggested journalists, like translators, are under constant time pressures. Deadlines get shorter and the amount of copy required for printing, the microphone or the camera gets ever longer. It is to be expected that short cuts become the rule rather than an exception. All of this relates to original documents in important way. Rather than return to primary sources when trying to understand how a story began which is what all thoughtful, discriminating and independent journalists were taught to do, they are tempted simply to pick over the bones of what their colleagues have already written.

This was a lesson that was impressed on me very early in my broadcasting career by my first editor. 'Don't bother with the books – there isn't time. Send for the press cuttings.' So I would ring up the 'morgue' and ask them to wheel out the dead bodies of whatever story I was hoping to revive as it had already been reported, and never mind the books, the official reports etc. Without labouring the point the danger here is that the journalist who chooses to source his/her story from news cuttings rather than primary sources runs the risk of simply repeating both the factual errors and the ill-informed judgements of his/her predecessors. Now a good many of those errors and judgements may have been the result of bad journalism, but equally it is possible that they flowed from inexactitudes in the original translation.

How much better for everyone concerned if the original translated document had been easily accessible, 'transparent' to use Arturo Tosi's description. Then it might have been a labour of love and not an unwelcome chore to ring up the library and ask for the original document or to log into the Internet and get back to basics.

I have perhaps painted a less than flattering picture of journalists at work and there *is* a sense in which many translators regard the mass media as the chief villains in the linguistic world. But it takes two to quarrel. A colleague of mine who works in radio has invented a word to describe the anti-European stance taken up by a number of the British newspapers. He calls them 'Eurolibels'. Those tales about 'straight' bananas or the death of cheese made from unpasteurised milk for example.

It occurs to me that many of these Eurolibels may have their source in what has often emerged as translation from the Commission in Brussels and, perhaps, the European Parliament too. In other words, those extraordinary, awkward sentences and those words and phrases so strange to many British ears that are used to describe the business of the EU may play a significant part in reinforcing an existing prejudice against Europe and all of its works. I appreciate that there must be a language that belongs to the business of the EU, that can be readily understood by all who are involved and which has an exact meaning. That ugly noun 'subsidiarity' is an example of that. However I would still maintain that language when it is used well is 'plain and unadorn'd'. It seeks simplicity without sacrificing complexity. To be fancy, it walks with the idea of truth and is therefore the enemy of prejudice.

If, in their hearts, journalists think that translators are pedants and translators know that journalists are really cowboys, there is also another way in which each group views the other. And it is equally unflattering, and equally unfair. Nevertheless journalists do regard translators as the language police and, for their part, the translators are convinced that journalists are linguistic burglars, robbing and stealing their way around the rules. But this is to suppose that in English – and it is only of English that I can write with any authority – the rules are set and settled, that language is a kind of stone from which each us carves what we need. However, the analogy that would occur to most journalists is not one to do with stone but with rubber. Language must be punched and pulled into shape in a personal way if it is to be fashioned into anything that has meaning for readers, listeners and viewers. And in attempting to shape that slippery rubber the practitioner constantly negotiates his or her way through all the varieties of existing English and other languages too, taking, borrowing and stealing whatever helps to communicate.

Thus if we believe that language precedes culture, that indeed language is culture, then it is fair to say that the journalist is a vital part of the process by which culture shifts and changes. I would suspect that this is very much how translators also see their role in society. In this sense, if none of the others that I have already written about, translators and journalists have more in common that they are prepared to recognise. By the same token each has much to teach the other.

## Chapter 10

# Linguistic Interpenetration or Cultural Contamination?

HELEN SWALLOW

Workshop 1, on linguistic aspects of multilingualism, with special reference to lexical contacts and borrowings across languages, brought together a public consisting mainly of translators – some hundred in number – from the European Parliament's Translation Directorate. Native speakers of all the EU's 11 official languages were therefore present. The first speaker made the important observation that this was a forum in which he could not use his mother tongue (Portuguese), but was faced with a choice between two foreign languages (French and English). He went on to alternate between these two languages, providing a neat embodiment of the subject of the day's seminar.

The subject matter that emerged and was aired at the workshop can be summed up under a number of headings: the role and influence of the translator; pressures on the translator (including the pressure of dealing with neologisms); the fine line between linguistic innovation and conservatism which translators tread; possible ways of helping translators to face these challenges; and, finally and relatedly, the pressures on the Union's languages.

The role and influence of the translator were brought up early in the debate by a Greek colleague, who said that it had occurred to him that many languages owe their very first literary written text to a translation; Luther's translation of the Gospels, for example, laid the foundations for the modern German language. Translations have thus, at various times, not only played the role of mediator but also had an influence on the receiving language, the mother tongue of the translator. In the case of the smaller languages, such as Greek, the translations in the European Parliament and other EU institutions represent an enormous number of structured, written, rigorous texts running into tens of thousands of pages per year. These texts, inevitably, have an influence on the Greek language spoken in the homeland. Translators should therefore keep an awareness, at least in the back of their minds, that they contribute to the shaping of their own mother tongue, giving emphasis not only to the contact between translator and author, but also to the contact between the translator and the user – or consumer – of the translated text.

The concept of translators as the 'guardians of language' was raised again, but only to be rejected. The word 'guardian' was seen as implying a closed attitude, whereas openness was considered more desirable: the speaker expressed a wish to act not as a guardian but as a host(ess), welcoming new words with open arms, neologisms representing as they do new blood for the language (on condition, however, that it is not 'contaminated' blood).

Opinion was divided as to whether it was the role of the translator to add something new to a text, making translation a somewhat (although not excessively) creative process, or whether translators, even if they spot mistakes or sloppiness in the original, should refrain from intervening, following the principle that their job is to translate, not to improve on, the original text.

The possibility of texts for translation being marred by 'mistakes or sloppiness' leads on to the second theme: the pressures on translators. One of these was seen as being the sometimes inferior quality, in linguistic terms, of the texts received for translation.

One possible reason for this was the use of a lingua franca, in practice usually English or French, for drafting parliamentary amendments, for example, with none of the authors actually writing in their mother tongue. A similar situation might arise if, for any one of a number of practical reasons, texts were drafted by a single author in a language other than his or her own. This could place translators, often working under time pressure, in a difficult situation. Sometimes, if translators were able to make contact with the text's originator, they could play a part in improving the quality of the original, thus contributing to the creative process. If not, as the chairman of the workshop, Barry Wilson, Director-General of the European Parliament's Directorate-General for Translation and General Services, pointed out, this could lead to the paradoxical situation of up to ten high-quality translations being adopted as official documents in parallel with a linguistically flawed original. (If time permitted, it would perhaps be best if every original were sent to the translation division in question for revision, as is already done with parliamentary written questions.)

The view that less-than-perfect drafting was confined to those not writing in their mother tongue was forcefully challenged by another speaker, who said the following:

It was mentioned that the authors of texts who did not write in their mother tongue should indicate [that this is the case]. I do not think that it will make much difference. One of the problems is that the 4000 people involved in the European Parliament are probably one of the biggest sources of linguistic contamination in Europe, because they talk to each other a lot, very often on subjects that are in a preparatory state and, therefore, have not been translated yet. So they talk about it, having read it in whichever language it happens to be [drafted] in, and therefore there will be either a lot of French loan words or a lot of English loan words, and what comes out of it is a complete mishmash, linguistically speaking. We get a lot of questions – written questions and questions for Question Time – written by native speakers with a lot of not only loan words, but, let us say, very unusual grammatical structures and things like that. So I do not think the principle of native speakers necessarily guarantees that it is good quality.

Linked to this is another pressure faced by translators at the European Parliament – the fact that they too are in what the same speaker went on to describe as 'this linguistic cesspool', and that they have to steer a very difficult course between taking on board a lot of loan words, even though they might be precise, or becoming too conservative. This was seen as being especially true of the more – geographically – peripheral languages. It might be easier for French or German people to stay in close contact with the development of their language via the media, whereas it was more difficult for the Greeks, Portuguese, Danes, Finns and Swedes, because they had no daily contact with their languages. The speaker believed that what should be done was simply to choose the media in the Member States that make a conscious effort to write good Danish or good Swedish, and try to follow them, rather than just jumping on an English loan word used in some tabloid or specialist magazine and saying 'We can use that here as well'. Some time should be allowed to elapse to see if the loan word established itself in the more serious communicative media.

The chairman thought that it was probably wise to take this line, while at the same time retaining a certain openness to the development of language. We should neither set ourselves up as an academy which would protect some false integrity or imagined pure language nor should we be totally promiscuous. Finding that line, he supposed, was one of the things for which we were paid.

In the same context, a Greek translator put forward the view that the translation divisions in the European Parliament and the Commission tended to be rather more conservative and rather more normative than writers in the homeland who were in contact with current linguistic developments (what another speaker had termed 'market forces'). They were a little less bold, a little more purist and a little more reluctant to use a foreign term which might have come into current usage in Greece, possibly having come into being in a less than academic setting. This could represent a slight danger and could end in the situation described at the morning's session by Arturo Tosi, where two versions of an EU document existed side by side – the official one and the popular one.

The same speaker made some practical proposals as to how this situation might be remedied. One would be to use the possibilities offered by information technology to set up informal contacts between Luxembourg, Brussels and the Member States, and informal networks of qualified users of the language in the Member States. Another possibility would be to enable translators, after eight or ten years in Luxembourg, to work for a month or two in their home country on detachment to a ministry or a current affairs journal, for example. This should not be regarded as a perk or a paid holiday, but as an opportunity for translators to refresh their knowledge by immersing themselves in the language actually being used in their home country. This would be especially relevant for nationalities which had no access to television in their own language in Luxembourg. (The chairman mentioned that the interpreters' service at the Commission had just such a scheme; it was known as '_ressourcement_'.)

The subjects of lexical borrowing (usually from English) and neologisms were raised by a number of speakers, sometimes with illustrations ('airbag' and 'mainstreaming', for example) taken from the European Parliament's terminological database Euterpe.

One speaker mentioned the difference between past and present-day lexical borrowing. In the past one language might borrow from another because the receiving language lacked either the technology or the knowledge to invent a term of its own, as in the case of Latin borrowing terms from Greek in fields such as geography and philosophy. In the modern world the situation is rather different. There is hardly a country in the world which lacks basic knowledge in any given subject. Sometimes there is a need to create a new term because a new product has come onto the market. However, because it is so easy to communicate in real time throughout the world, an engineer in India will have the same background as one in the United States.

The same speaker also made a point concerning what he termed 'negative loans'. By this he meant the kind of terms that came into being when the content of a science was filtered and mediated by the knowledge and specialised competence of a particular translator. In many case these were not so much translations as 'spot solutions' – the terms that translators came up with when they lacked either the time or the knowledge to find the correct term. This often took the form of the translator using the hypernym – the more generic term instead of the proper, more precise, one. He cited the example of 'financial controller', which in the European Parliament is rendered in Italian as *controllore finanziario*, when the proper term would be *revisore contabile*; the dictionary definition of *revisore contabile* contains the terms *controllore finanziario*, suggesting that translators have a tendency to use the nearest generic definition because they are not acquainted with a particular sense of a word. This is the danger of not having specialised people to translate specialised subjects. As John Trim had said, there was a sort of convergence between languages, resulting in a loss in richness of vocabulary.

Another contributor suggested that 'contamination' between languages has its roots in the specialised nature of modern education. In the past, scientists, engineers and all educated people had a very strong classical linguistic background, which enabled them to find expressions for concepts, old and new, rather than simply transposing a foreign term into their language. Now engineers and scientists have a technical background, so that they understand the concepts very well, but they are either unable or reluctant to express them correctly in their language for fear that they might say something completely different from what is said, for example, in the American magazines, and thus risk being misunderstood.

It was suggested by another speaker that there should be input from linguists when neologisms were being created – a kind of 'linguistically assisted creation of neologisms' along the lines of 'medically assisted procreation'.

Towards the end of the debate the chairman asked the question: 'Are you, as translators, afraid of English?' The question provoked laughter, but also some considered responses.

The first respondent said that he was not afraid, for the simple reason that in many cases the English term might have another connotation from that of an apparent synonym already existing in the receiving language or might belong to a different register. It is well known that no two words are perfectly synonymous: sometimes because they collocate differently with verbs or adjectives; sometimes because they are used in a different context, with a different audience. In the case of some other English loan words in Italian, 'benchmarking' and 'empowerment' for example, there is no satisfactory translation. These words can be seen in the Italian financial papers every day, which means that they are regarded as specific to the sector in which they are used. A translation would not reflect the specialised connotation that the English word has and would probably be misunderstood by specialist readers.

It was felt by another speaker that we do not yet have the distance in time to judge whether the influx of English words into other languages will be an enrichment or not. Greek, for example, has many loan words: when Greece gained its independence in the 19th century its vocabulary contained many Turkish and Italian words, so a need was felt to create Greek equivalents, and this was done. The existence of doublets or triplets did not impoverish the language, but enriched it – since language abhors total synonymy, the onetime synonyms came to acquire different connotations. At the moment the influx of English is so rapid and so recent that it is not possible to judge whether the same will happen with the present phenomenon.

A German contributor said that, while not afraid of any form of multilingualism, he was afraid in some cases of being overwhelmed. In some parts of the German-language cultural area this was happening, but it was being caused, ironically, by some German speakers themselves, who so much embraced and preferred English or American culture that they thought it appropriate to impose the English language on their fellow countrymen. This resulted in a highly adulterated form of German, which he sometimes did not recognise as his own language. When walking through the streets of Hamburg, for instance, he felt estranged because so many shops had English names and showcases whose contents had English labels. This was the result of a certain class of people not wanting others to share their form of communication. Such phenomena had, of course, also occurred in the Baroque period, when the gentry in most European countries would converse in French; but at least some of them had really studied French, and could hold learned discussions or sing songs in real French. What was encountered nowadays was bits of English being thrown around in no particular order.

In a different context, there was a case before an industrial tribunal in Frankfurt in which an engineer had been dismissed by the airline for which he worked for using German words rather than English ones in reports to his superiors. (This was not in an area such as air traffic control where English had to be used for safety reasons, which the speaker fully accepted.)

Much ground had been covered in this discussion among translators, normally a category, in the words of one speaker, 'more accustomed to the shadows than the limelight'. Conclusions were not reached, but many questions were asked, questions which, as the group's spokesman said in her final report to the assembly, remain open for discussion and reflection.

John Trim, when asked by the chairman to give his final thoughts on the debate, said:

> It is, of course, very difficult to intervene when one is an English native speaker. What I say is likely to be immediately discredited by the source from which it comes. I think it is very important to understand why rather than simply deplore. People usually, one way or another, have good reasons for doing what they do, and we need to understand what they are doing and why they are doing it. There may be a functional reason, which is not simply discreditable. […] English is the latest in a long series of languages which have had this kind of intrusive effect upon others. When we look back on the others we do not find them, for the most part, to have been so threatening after all.

## Chapter 11

# Equivalences or Divergences in Legal Translation?

NICOLE BUCHIN and EDWARD SEYMOUR

## Introduction

The papers contributed by members of Workshop 2 explored and illustrated the principle that translation cannot be regarded as a
straightforward, neutral process. Any act of translation involves making a
choice, which means taking decisions; in the case of legislative or political
documents the decision acquires a legislative or political dimension as
well. For this reason it would be desirable for all those involved in drafting
multilingual texts, including the translators, to interact throughout the
process, so as to ensure that the will of the legislator or politician finds
equivalent expression in each of the 11 official languages.

Is Euro-jargon useful, or is it merely a lazy and unreadable way of
creating 'equivalent' texts? Francisco Peyró argued that although *acquis
communautaire* was now enshrined in the treaties, it was unintelligible
outside the Community context and should be used with caution even
when addressed only to Community readers. Erika Landi said the legal
harmonisation resulting from adoption of the *Corpus Juris* in the field of
criminal law would also involve linguistic harmonisation, to define 'equivalent' terms. The *Corpus* had been translated outside the Community
context; it would need revising to harmonise its terminology. While some
terms were already used in the language's national law, others introduced
innovative concepts. This readjustment of national terminology might be
described as the task of multilingual correspondence; it would include
eliminating the ambiguities in some language versions. Supplementing her
comments, Antonio Tilotta said criminal law was a new challenge for Parliament. The points his group had selected were a few of the linguistic
issues raised by this major undertaking, such as the need for harmonised

equivalents to 'accusé'. They might be settled in a series of collation meetings.

Bjarne Sørensen summarised the contributions in his subgroup, dealing with the *codecision procedure,* the complexity of which gave rise to particular linguistic hazards. Individual papers illustrated the problem by referring to the case of 'designs and models', 'sustainable development' and 'universal and public service'. He postulated the existence of a 'linguistic subsidiarity principle', by which national usage might have to override Community convenience. The practical advantages of changing the 'original language' in the course of a document's history outweighed the linguistic disadvantages. Areas for future progress (which Helmut Spindler confirmed were already being explored) included cooperation between the different institutions' language services, secondment of linguists to the committees and closer contact with the Minutes Department.

Introducing his case study on the *political impact* of translation, Edward Seymour suggested that the biblical authority of the term 'democratic accountability' had frightened off attempts to find a figure of speech that was easier to translate. Writers drafting in a foreign language needed linguistic assistance at the start, while native writers might have to adopt a 'European dialect'.

Olaf Pries' point on 'anti-people mines' drew attention to ideological differences as the source of problems with terminology, especially when the translator did not share the author's views. In Gudrun Haller's discussion of *Mitbestimmung,* the lack of legal equivalence in other languages and the politically sensitive character of the closest equivalent terms in other languages – such as *participation* in French – made translation difficult in such contexts as the European Community. Political sensitivity had also precluded consistent translation in the case of 'Macedonia', as Maria Bali demonstrated. In her discussion on the 'legal implications of lexical choices in political discourse', Isabel Vale Majerus was looking for a match between political usage and legal meaning, affected neither by ideology nor by political correctness.

## Discussion

Launching the discussion, Ellen Parlow argued that jargon played a valuable role in translation, particularly where it created succinct terminology for complex ideas – as in the case of 'acquis communautaire'; Francisco Peyró said 'acquis' embodied the notion of irrevocability, whereas 'ordre juridique' did not. Filippo Vitanza thought the unbroken evolution of the EU explained why writers favoured 'acquis' rather than 'ordre'. Another speaker argued for greater responsibility in protecting languages – particularly the less dominant ones – from Community neologisms.

Edward Seymour drew attention to the interinstitutional guidelines on _drafting quality_, which were currently being discussed by Parliament's Legal Affairs Committee and proposed setting up 'drafting units' to ensure that texts were translatable. Frank Wohlgemuth agreed with Renato Correia that if authors (and particularly lawyers) recognised the drafting responsibility of translators they would provide much more guidance with their texts. Wilhelmus Hillhorst thought we also had a multinational responsibility, not only to reconcile linguistic differences between countries with a common language but also to discourage neologisms influenced by the dominant languages. In the case of the codecision procedure, he agreed with Bjarne Sørensen on the need for more detailed linguistic information. Involving linguists or lawyer–linguists in the drafting of texts from the start was desirable, but would require greater coordination than at present.

Nicole Buchin agreed that Community jargon sometimes fulfilled a valuable purpose, but it should not be allowed to restrict or impoverish the national languages. The workshop's proposed conclusions should highlight the need for greater _coordination with authors_; closer involvement of translators in the drafting process; the problem of lexical choices imposed by other authors or institutions; and clearer definition of the prospective roles of translators, lawyer–linguists, the Minutes and the legal department. Wilhelmus Hilhorst saw greater involvement in the drafting process as a way of improving the quality of translation, while Olaf Pries thought more conspicuous translators would help to prevent the imposition of unsuitable terminology. Mechanisation, in another speaker's view, ought to increase translators' thinking time and thus enhance the readability of texts, but the use of jargon in translations suggested that any extra thinking time had been absorbed by the quickening pace of work. The introduction of IT had not, in Wilhelmus Hlihorst's view, led to a reduction of workload.

Francisco Peyró wondered why, if the lawyer–linguists were doing such a good job, the Court was having to consider so many cases of linguistic discrepancy. He had mentioned 12 such cases in his paper. Helmut Spindler agreed that this organisational aspect needed consideration.

Taking up the issue of drafting quality which Wilhelmus Hillhorst had raised, Renato Correia drew attention to a series of recent initiatives in this direction, none of which included translation as part of the process for optimising quality. This point is made in some detail in the conclusions, subsequently adopted by the seminar in plenary session.

## Conclusions

### Constraints

From the legal and linguistic points of view, the unique character of the historical process of European integration derives from its creation of a body of law in, at present, 11 official languages. The different language versions of this Community legislation – which in some cases applies directly to the Member States and their citizens, while in others it has to be transposed into the various national legal systems – must all, in theory, have the same legal value. However, it is worth drawing attention to the extensive case-law of the Court of Justice on divergences between language versions which are supposed to be equivalent. This principle of equivalence also applies, of course, to political statements of opinion adopted by Parliament and the other institutions.

Should the principle be applied by means of a linguistic exercise that is regarded as a simple transfer operation, from the language of an initial version into the other ten, an exercise that by cultural convention we call 'translation'? That is the main question to which the authors of our various contributions have endeavoured to provide partial, but complementary, answers.

### Main problems facing translators

A consideration of the case studies in our collection raises once again the major problems with which translators have to contend; as we all know, they concern not only the source text but also the context in which it is written, or in which the new language versions are expected to be used.

These include, for instance, phrasing that is unclear in its use of vocabulary or grammar, because the authors have not used their main language; inadvertent or deliberate ambiguity, the woolly language that expresses a political compromise; inconsistencies arising from changes in the draftsman's language between the various stages of a given procedure; and inconsistency between the terminology used in the EU and that of the Member States or international law.

Nor is our work made any easier by the intervention of other operators, particularly in the codecision procedure. Here one might mention the preference of one or more MEPs for choosing a given term at the successive stages of draft report or report, the Parliament Legal Service's opinions, the preferences of the various institutions during the conciliation stage and the *ex-post* intervention of lawyer–linguists or the Minutes Department.

Such intervention is quite legitimate and sometimes essential, but it does not always take account of the translator's active involvement in the process of drafting almost all of the various language versions.

## Improvements

The issues raised by multilingualism are becoming more and more pressing in the Union, especially as a result of Parliament's 'co-legislative' role, strengthened by the Treaty of Amsterdam, and in the prospect of enlargement. Both Parliament[1] and the European Council[2], as well as other institutions and bodies, have acknowledged the importance of linguistic diversity in the Union and the principle of equality between all the Union's official languages.

Those issues are now more clearly understood. For example, a Declaration (No. 39) on the quality of the drafting of Community Legislation[3] was annexed to the Final Act of the Treaty of Amsterdam. It has duly encouraged efforts to improve both the form and substance of Community legislation. They include the Commission document *Better Lawmaking*[4], which has prompted two reports by the Legal Affairs Committee, one on formal quality[5] and the other on substantial quality[6].

In the same spirit, an inter-institutional group of representatives from the legal departments of Parliament, the Council and the Commission has drawn up 'Draft Common Guidelines on the Quality of Drafting of Community Legislation'[7], in accordance with Declaration 39 mentioned earlier.

Finally, we should not forget the report by Mr Manzella, on behalf of the Committee on Institutional Affairs, on the new codecision procedure after Amsterdam.[8] The proposals it contains deal particularly with improving the legal quality of parliamentary texts at first reading. There should be time for checking the legal and linguistic quality of amendments at the first stage of the procedure, which is bound to impinge on the translator's role (affecting not only translators, but also lawyer–linguists and the Minutes department). It adds the requirement to provide a written justification for every legislative amendment by Parliament, which should make translation easier as it will clarify the author's intention.

The reforms also consider the importance of terminology: in the words of the common guidelines,

- Draft Community acts should be framed in terms which reflect the multilingual nature of Community legislation; concepts or terminology specific to any given national legal system should be used with caution.
- The terminology used in a given act should be consistent both internally and with existing Community acts, especially those relating to the same fields.
- Identical concepts should be expressed in the same terms, as far as possible without departing from their meaning in ordinary, legal or technical language.

The purpose of these reforms is to ensure that Community legislation is properly understood by the general public and, more particularly, by those for whom it is intended, so that Community law is uniformly applied throughout the Member States. However, they do not go far enough. It is desirable that the role of translation as an integral part of Parliament's activity should be fully recognised, which – to judge by the documents cited earlier – does not yet appear to be the case. People who request translations, and others involved in the legislative process, should cooperate with translators as closely as possible, particularly by providing translators with the information they require. More specifically, with regard to 'implementing measures' (c) and (d) recommended in the draft common guidelines of the three institutions, terminologists and translators must participate in the 'drafting units' and follow the courses of 'training in legal drafting' designed for writers.

Proposals have been made in various quarters for improving cooperation between the departments involved in drafting parliamentary texts. To ensure that they take practical effect, it would in our view be necessary to change the mind-set in which the suggested measures are carried out. In other words, it would require all those concerned with drafting multilingual texts, whether they are legislative or political in intent, to regard translation as a constituent part of the drafting process.

## Notes

1. Resolution on the use of the official languages in the European Union, OJ C 43, 20.2.1995, p. 91.
2. See especially the conclusion of the Cannes European Council of 26 and 27 June 1995, stressing the importance of linguistic diversity in the European Union,
3. Adopted by the Intergovernmental Conference of 2 October 1997.
4. COM(97)0620 – C4–0656/97 of 26 November 1997.
5. Report by Mrs Palacio Vallelersundi on a draft interinstitutional agreement on the quality of the drafting of legislative texts, A4–0498/98 of 9 December 1998.
6. Report by Mr Cot on the Commission's annual report (1997) to the European Council – 'Better lawmaking 1997', A4–0460/98 of 26 November 1998.
7. PE 228.137 of 3 September 1998, CM\359143; the guidelines were adopted on 22 December 1998 and published in the *Official Journal,* OJ C 73, 17.3.1999, p. 1.
8. A4–0271/98 of July 1998.

## Chapter 12

# *Opaque or User-friendly Language?*

CHRISTOPHER ROLLASON

Workshop 3 was chaired by John Loydall, with the participation of Arturo Tosi and Christopher Cook, and of representatives from the individual language divisions of Parliament's Translation Service and its terminology section. The discussion focused on the question of the accessibility of Parliament's documents – that is, their comprehensibility for the general public and the role of the translator in facilitating that accessibility. This summary is based on the proceedings of the session of the Workshop on 26 November 1998, enriched where pertinent by a number of points which arose at the group's preparatory meetings.

Parliament's language service has a major responsibility, namely to make multilingualism work in practice. The central problem may be described as the *quality of communication:* the public is obviously entitled to expect readable, intelligible and 'user-friendly' texts from the EU institutions. There are, however, obstacles to communication: the source documents are not always unequivocally clear, as they are the end-product of compromises between different national policies; another enemy of clarity is cross-contamination between languages. All this can lead to a public perception in the Member States of EU texts as being opaque.

As far as Parliament's documents are concerned, one of the main user communities is the press. Journalists want to have access to texts that explain the work of Parliament in a concise and understandable form. A wide range of documentation is in fact available to both press and public – the verbatim record of Parliament's debates (the *CRE* or *compte rendu in extenso*), the texts of reports distributed before each Strasbourg sitting, brochures aimed at the general public, and the *News Report* produced by Parliament's press service – but the existence of these sources is not always sufficiently publicised. As a result, in some Member States there is a feeling that the public is not adequately informed about what Parliament does. However, translators cannot themselves influence the question of physical

117

access to documents; such access is, in any case, now swiftly becoming far easier thanks to the Internet. Notably, the texts of reports can now be read on the Parliament's website, as can the *CRE*, in its multilingual and translated versions.

Improved access to documents, even with all the marvels of communications technology, does not in itself ensure that the documents will be understood. However, the translator is not in a position to alter the basic terminology of EU institutions, which in any case corresponds to a specifically *European reality*, itself in a constant process of creation. Terms which might appear to be mere political jargon in fact very often have a specific technical sense or else correspond to precise objectives laid down in the Treaties. From the legal perspective, the need for a uniform body of Community law applying in all the Member States does not leave much leeway for terminological variation. In any case, the whole is greater than the sum of its parts: the European reality is not and cannot be identical to any of the individual realities of' the Member States, as it involves the creation of qualitatively new phenomena, of a transnational nature, that have no direct precedents or equivalents. From this perspective, the gap between Union and Member State terminology can even be viewed as a linguistic enrichment. Terminology should not be seen as something to be afraid of: no branch of human activity can function without a certain number of technical terms, which together make up a 'technolect'. Where it is in the perceived interest of members of the public to familiarise themselves with EU language, they have proved perfectly willing to do so; a case in point is the intimate knowledge of the CAP displayed by farmers in some Member States. On the other hand, some European languages are, for a host of cultural reasons, more permeable to loan-words than others, and translators and terminologists should be aware of this factor when faced with the task of introducing new terms in their own languages to correspond to the EU's new realities.

It is not the role of the translator to explain Parliament's political positions or render them accessible to the public; those tasks fall to such 'multipliers' as Parliament's own press and public relations services and the newspapers and other media. Equally, it is not the business of the translator to rewrite the text: translators are not multipliers, but mediators. It is the responsibility of the author to ensure that a text is transparent. In this connection, an important new factor in the EU equation is the 'open government' *culture of accessibility* that exists in Sweden and Finland: in these Member States, it is expected that official documents will be understandable by everyone. It also appears that in these two countries there is more interest on the part of the general public in consulting official documents (national or European) than in many of the 'older' Member States. This 'Nordic' approach could be more widely adopted in order to encourage greater linguistic transparency in Union matters generally. There may be a good case for rewriting the entire body of EU law in order to simplify it but any such policy would not be a decision of the translation services. However, if the declared target were accessibility, that would have to imply *translatability* – a goal which can only be achieved on a basis of integration between authors and translators. Such a goal would also require greater awareness on the translators' part of the specific cultural traditions of each of the Member States: only in this way can the European message be put across successfully.

What then can the translator do? One way of improving things would be to render the text in a more accessible style and a simpler syntax (following the 'Nordic' model), but this also requires goodwill on the author's part. Also desirable would be closer cooperation between translator and author, in the context of a fuller integration of the communication process.

It would, further, be helpful for translators to be aware of the limits of all the European languages, their own included. No living European language was designed when it came into being to deal with today's common European context. Translators should bear in mind the need to distinguish between the different national traditions: in some Member States, priority is given to maintaining the integrity of' the national language against external influences, whereas in others the emphasis is placed on communication. Translation at the European level should aim to reconcile both local and international perspectives, as part of the greater task of encouraging the creation – and the public acceptance, in all our Member States – of a common European home.

# Chapter 13

# *Round Table on Multilingualism: Barrier or Bridge?*

SYLVIA BALL

The conference round table or panel discussion is too well known an art form to need much introduction. Its aim is always to allow participants to react to each other's presentations and to give other members of the round table the chance to give their impressions of the proceedings, in the case in point as linguists and/or communicators. The participants in the Multilingualism Seminar Round Table, which was chaired by Barry Wilson, Director-General of Translation and General Services at the European Parliament (EP), were the morning's two guest speakers, John Trim and Arturo Tosi, Christopher Cook of the BBC, Olga Cosmidou, Director of Interpretation at the EP, Colette Flesch, Director-General of the European Commission's Translation Service, and Malou Lindholm, MEP.

All the round table contributors had relevant, important and interesting points to make, but it has to be said that the audience hit of the morning was one of the first speak, the Swedish MEP Malou Lindholm. She began her speech with a graphic account of the problems faced by MEPs from new countries – even those with more than respectable language skills – with a mass of multilingual documentation to assimilate and a shortage of both interpreters and translators for their languages. Sometimes the problem was one of sheer availability of any translation or interpretation at all, sometimes it was a matter of buck-passing, when institutions refused to translate texts from the past for which they considered others responsible, sometimes the problem was one of receiving translations in time to analyse and understand the information they contained, and be prepared to act upon it. It was very difficult to table amendments to a report when the deadline for doing so meant that the report itself was not yet available in your own language. All three problems, particularly unrealistic deadlines, feature largely – and negatively – in the EP translators' life and they could therefore be expected to receive the message sympathetically, but it was Malou Lindholm's next point which brought the greatest applause, the importance of having texts, particularly legal texts, translated in-house rather than externally, because of the greater accuracy, precision and general comprehensibility of the former as opposed to the latter.

The extent of the audience's enthusiasm can only be understood against the background of the period in which the seminar took place. One way of containing the costs of a EU set to almost double in size over the next decade is indeed to send more work out for freelance translation, on the face of it at least a less expensive option than recruiting staff translators. In the mid-to-late 1990s the EP's Translation Service had accordingly been cooperating with other EU institutions to organise calls for tender for freelance translation services, an unpopular option with full-time staff, who saw this less as a threat to their own position than a time-wasting exercise in proving the obvious point that highly-skilled, experienced translators selected by open competition are more competent at the task than outsiders. Some EP staff present had become aware of this as assessors and quality controllers of freelance test translations. Others were translation managers who had been faced with the double problem of receiving inadequate freelance translations and having to assign them for revision in-house to staff translators, who did not hesitate to express their lack of satisfaction with the task. All were delighted to have their feelings so eloquently confirmed by one of their political 'masters', in the presence of their own top management.

The top manager present, Barry Wilson, could not resist the opportunity to respond to Malou Lindholm, although at the beginning of the seminar he had said that he would not express his opinions. Interestingly, however, he made no attempt to dispute her negative assessment of external translation, concentrating instead on the need for all parties to the translation process to accept and respect deadlines. It is indeed true that, in a political institution, even at the highest level you cannot repeat too often the message that 'the fact of working in 11 languages has some constraints and that the timetable of parliamentary work has to take that into account'. Even if you then have to conclude as Barry Wilson did that 'that is an impossible dream'.

However, it would be wrong to assume that the round table was concerned solely – or even mainly – with matters internal to the EP. The external guests ensured that the discussion was wide ranging and focused on issues of general importance. It was Christopher Cook, the BBC radio journalist, who had been the first speaker called on by the chairman to give his views of the proceedings so far. Since they are expressed in another paper in this volume (see pp. 99–103), it is unnecessary to enlarge on them here. It is enough to point out that one of his main points was the need for European institutions and their staff, particularly translators, to be aware of the many and varied national needs of those receiving their message in the Member States. In reply, Colette Flesch had used the example of documentation for the European elections, produced in a decentralised way so that it could be focused on the interests of European citizens at the local and regional level to show that, whatever the outside perception of the institutions, this could indeed be the case.

Another important theme of the round table was the importance, both on the practical and the idealistic level, of improving consciousness of Europe – what Arturo Tosi would later call European awareness – in the Member States and the countries which are currently candidates for EU accession. To take the practical contribution first, it was made in a spirited address by the EP's Director of Interpretation, Olga Cosmidou. Drawing on the experience of successive enlargements of the European Communities from the six countries with four official languages of the 1950s (and these languages all more or less widely taught) to the 15-country, 11-language EU of the late 1990s and the likelihood of an even larger Union in the early 21st century with many working languages which were not widely known, she advocated the reorganisation of national education systems to make it easier for new members to be assimilated. It was, she felt, short-sighted for new Member States to insist on their language being immediately represented in the translation or interpretation service when they had made little effort to ensure that their country was in possession of sufficient linguists with the right skills to be able to do so. In general young Europeans were able to learn only the same few languages – English, French and, to a more limited extent, German, Spanish and Italian – but how could a language become a working language of the EU if the country's school system was not rethought to take account of Europe and, in particular, its linguistic diversity?

In his contribution a little later John Trim took up Olga Cosmidou's points about the need to Europeanise the national education systems of the EU and used them to develop a broader vision of the European educational and linguistic ideal. While recognising the contribution of the development of the nation state to universal education, he criticised the oppression of national minorities inherent in such an approach, saying that 'schools ... ha[d] been designed to make the knowledge of the standard language of the State a universal means of communication and [of] accession to the power of the State'. However, what was now needed was the transformation of the national system into a means of European education in the most profound sense, an ideal that was far from being a reality. He looked forward to a time when subjects would be taught not only in a variety of

European languages but also by staff drawn from countries across Europe and when children would view school as a European rather than a purely national institution. Of course he recognised that what he was calling for was '*Zukunftsmusik*', that such a change in attitudes would be possible only in the long term, but a start could be made by liberalising the teaching profession in the same way that other professions had been, so that there were no barriers to teacher mobility.

John Trim went on to make a further point illustrating his commitment to the multilingual, multicultural European ideal, starting from the need to recognise unconscious language skills. How could somebody in Germany who had learned English claim to have no knowledge of Dutch, since all three languages were so close? How could an Italian who had learned French claim to know no Portuguese? How could any European fail to see how much Greek he knew? People needed to be encouraged to use their intelligence and their common sense to make sense of texts in languages that they were not aware of understanding. He then described, to the audience's delight, a Council of Europe workshop where participants had listened to an interview in Finnish and used it to discover their latent knowledge of the language and its grammar. To an audience of EU translators, many of whom had recently had to grapple with the task of learning precisely that language chosen by the workshop organisers for its surface impenetrability, the joke was too good to be missed. But John Trim's point, that 'part of education in European languages should be to convince people that our languages are all human languages, spoken by people like us to express meanings of the sort that are important and accessible to all of us', deserves to be inscribed on the European equivalent of Christopher Cook's 'empty chair' (see p. 99). It would be an important breakthrough if national audiences were to realise that they are Europeans too. Who knows? If this were to be understood by the British media it might even counter the occasional 'Eurolibel' (see p. 102).

In the last part of his speech John Trim combined the practical with the visionary. In practical terms he described the efforts being made in the framework of the Council of Europe's proposed European Year of Languages in 2001 to launch a European Language Portfolio which would encourage children to express their experiences in as many languages as possible and count all language knowledge as a worthwhile acquisition, even if it was not sanctioned by formal qualifications. On the visionary level, his closing words are worth quoting verbatim:

> We should not think in terms of big languages and little languages, that big languages matter and little languages do not, that people who speak them have to learn the rest and nobody else need bother with

them. We should try to get some kind of reciprocity and a feeling of being part of this Community and living together.

It was an understandably popular conclusion for an audience of convinced Europeans where there were at least as many native speakers of 'little languages' as of 'big languages' and where the speakers of the latter had a commitment to the importance and relevance of the former, as the mother tongues of many of their colleagues and, indeed, as the languages they themselves translated from.

Nonetheless, since events like the multilingualism seminar do not take place in a vacuum, it is important to situate the debate about 'big' and 'little' languages, as well as the need for countries which wish to join the EU to prepare by ensuring they have a suitable pool of linguists to provide the EU institutions with translators and interpreters, in the context of the EU institutions and their debate about the organisational changes required for future enlargements. Olga Cosmidou had been the first to raise the issue, speaking about the costs – in human as much as in budgetary terms – of the efforts needed to build Europe. For interpreters, although nobody said so openly at the seminar, the human costs include the need to prepare for the influx of such a large number of additional languages that it might be necessary to envisage practices which have previously been rejected as unacceptable, such as working *into* two languages (i.e. a second language as well as their own mother tongue) or what Michael Smith[1] of *The Financial Times* would later call a hub-and-spoke system, in which speeches are first interpreted into one or two pivot languages (inevitably the 'big' ones) and only then into the rarer ones, an extension of the relay system already used on occasion by the European institutions. It was the relay system, of course, which was responsible for the notorious 1970s joke about the Danes always laughing last since, as Olga Cosmidou had reminded the seminar, theirs had been the first language to give the European Communities a real shock in terms of linguistic resources. In the early days, if there was nobody available to interpret directly from French or Italian into Danish, it was done in relay via English or German, with an inevitable delay so that whenever a speaker made a joke the Danish audience got the point a littler later than everybody else.

The danger of such situations recurring, of 'losing nuances' as Jean-Pierre Cot[2] was quoted as admitting in Michael Smith's article, is a very real one, but is there an alternative? The problem for the EP, where all languages are used in parliamentary business, is one of the exponential growth of the number of possible language combinations as the EU expands. The first wave of enlargement in the 21st century is likely to take the Union from 15 countries with 11 languages, i.e. 110 language combinations, to 21 countries[3] with 16 languages, some 240 combinations, and a future prospect of 22 languages with 462 language combinations. According to Smith, if the EP were to continue with the current interpretation system it would require 110 interpreters in 22 booths, which would outstretch the accommodation available in either Brussels or Strasbourg.[4] Of course, although nobody is suggesting that EP translators, whose work has a more permanent character than an interpreter's, should work into a language other than their own, the system of hub-and-spoke, or pivot, languages carries the same dangers of translations 'losing nuances' – particularly for political texts which may have an intentionally ambiguous dimension. This can be difficult enough to preserve when translating directly. What price ambiguity, other than the unintentional type criticised by Malou Lindholm, when translating a translation?

The practical question of the need to plan ahead for future enlargement was taken up by Colette Flesch, with her experience of heading the Commission's Translation Service during the previous enlargement process and the current contacts with the Central and Eastern European countries (CEECs) which have applied to join the EU in the early years of the 21st century. She pointed out, as Olga Cosmidou had already done for the 1995 enlargement, that adding a number of languages which were not widely known would present a great challenge both for the Union and for the countries concerned, because of the lack of the necessary language skills. However, she was optimistic. The educational systems inside the EU had already begun to think about revising their curricula to add new languages, and the Commission had begun to contact schools and universities in the candidate countries to show them what would be required and help them adapt. There was even funding available from Community programmes to improve language skills in the candidate countries. The EU institutions had also learned from their experience of previous disorganised enlargements and, by the time of the Finnish and Swedish accession, offices had been set up in advance in the countries concerned to organise the translation of the existing Community legislation, the *acquis communautaire*. They certainly intended to follow a similar procedure for the CEECs, which had already received funding from the Commission's TAIEX[4] task force to start on the same translation task.

It is premature to draw any conclusions about which will prove to be correct, Olga Cosmidou's questioning of the current approach as short sighted (she had suggested ostrich-like), or Colette Flesch's brisk optimism that after the problems and hesitations of the past, this time the institutions have got it right – Goldilock's enlargement, as it were. That would be a more suitable subject for a seminar round table discussion in 2008 than the present day, although with translators from 22 languages it would probably have to be held in the Euro-equivalent of the Albert Hall!

As is the way with meetings where visionary views are developed by those who feel passionately about them, the 1998 seminar Round Table was starting to run out of time, leaving only a brief period for Christopher Cook to respond to John Trim's idealistic speech and for Arturo Tosi, in closing the session, to make two new brief points about the existence of a translation culture specific to the European institutions and the media's role in educating the public about it, in changing attitudes to the problems and challenges of translation in a multilingual environment.

The first point is true enough, since the European institutions taken together employ several thousand translators[6] with, very largely, a common vision of their role as mediators of the institutions' business to the citizens of the Union. We could all agree with the mission statement of our Swedish colleagues at the EP that our job is to ensure that 'Swedish[7] members shall have access in all given situations and in good time to a document in their language which is correct in terms of content, style and terminology'. Arturo Tosi's second point, to my mind, is more problematic. Can the way the national media present translation be divorced from the way they present European issues in general? If the media are not willing or able to 'rectify [European citizens'] perception' of the respective roles of the institutions and the fact that it is institutions representing national interests (and elected by voters in the individual Member States) who play a dominant part in the EU decision-making process, there can be little hope that they will convey a sympathetic view of translation. Damning 'Brussels' in a Eurolibel makes a better headline, as does damning Euro-speak.

It would be wrong to close the summing up of the round table on a negative note, even if some of the points of view expressed left me at least a little sceptical. It is always tempting to conclude bumper-sticker fashion: Radio journalists do it in sound bites; Interpreters want everybody to do it multilingually; Learned professors do it with breadth and vision, etc. But that, too, would be wrong, because it would be as much a caricature as the Eurolibels of which Christopher Cook complained. It is better to recall what an opportunity the seminar was for the institutions to stand back from what Olga Cosmidou called 'the day-to-day production machine' of translation and interpretation and think strategically about the changes of the past and their implications for the future. In doing so it was of inestimable value to have the input provided by the round table's outside guests to prevent the proceedings becoming too introspective. It was also, let us face it, great fun. Christopher Cook's contribution was a bravura performance. John Trim's approach to language teaching, while not terribly practical, would certainly liven up professional training at 8.30 on a Monday morning. Malou Lindholm's account of what it feels like to be a newbie MEP was also a most entertaining eye-opener for an audience most of whom were experienced enough to take the Parliament for granted most of the time. But, as Arturo Tosi said, it was awareness that was the key message: awareness of what it means to be a professional linguist, awareness of what it takes to get the message across to the citizen in the 'empty chair', awareness of the value 'of being part of this Community and living together', in John Trim's words.

## Notes

1999) Language gridlock fears grow as EU border widens, *The* 24 July (reproduced in the FT.com archive), a sympathetic and ticle which might well qualify as an 'anti-Eurolibel'.
the EP 1997–99 and chairman of the Bureau's Working Party sm.
ing the Czech Republic, Estonia, Hungary, Poland, Slovenia ugh Maltese would not become an EU language.
Flesch would suggest as she was leaving that the problem y 'build[ing] new buildings'.
nce Information Exchange.
by Michael Smith for the EP are 500 translators and 200 inter-nmission's translation service is larger. The *General Report on the ropean Union 1999* does not break the figures down into trans-reters, but gives a global total of 1903 linguists (p. 406). The s' language services are rather smaller.
ish, Greek, etc., according to translation division.

# Chapter 14

# *Conclusions*

ARTURO TOSI

This book about translation was written by translators and by people who work very closely with the world of EU translation. The debate in which they were involved (which started with a conference within the Translation Service of the European Parliament in 1998) and to which they contributed the papers published in this collection assumes particular significance today: it was the first time a large group of translators from different linguistic backgrounds had met to discuss multilingual translation in the EU and to voice their views on the institutional constraints affecting their work. In these closing remarks I stress the political dimension of multilingualism in the EU, and the professional role of the translator as communicator, on which much of European credibility, and the ambitious project of 'speaking with one voice in many languages', will ultimately depend.

   The two issues of official multilingualism and multilingual translation are closely intertwined, though traditionally neither politicians nor the researchers in the Community have examined this in much detail. An initial attempt to do so is, I hope, attained by this book, where the contributions analyse specific translation issues in connection with the linguistic and cultural implications of multilingualism. This is a useful and important change in perspective when attempting to establish consensus between professional and political circles. Such a consensus is now overdue: Europe's founders endorsed the principle of official multilingualism, but since then the Community has failed to reappraise language planning or language policy issues or the question of multilingual translation. This has led to a silent agreement whereby politicians have viewed translation as a technical matter and the translators have accepted an 'invisible role', though they have increasingly felt that the system did justice neither to themselves as writers of texts nor to the general public as readers of the different language versions.

   Some recent discussions regarding the founders' ruling that any given

European law should have equal legal status and validity, whatever EU language it might be written in, have highlighted the 'illusion of equivalence' between the different language versions of the piece of same legislation (Koskinen, 2000). Looking at the 'cultural turn' that has taken place in translation studies in the 1990s, Koskinen also points out that this revolution has passed quite unnoticed by the Commission's Translation Service. One explanation, she suggests, is that Europe is used to acultural communication, and hence documents that are meant to be applicable in all Member States must avoid culture-specific features. Another explanation that might perhaps account for the relative lack of institutional attention for the new cultural orientation of translation studies relates to the history of the Translation Service in the Community. The system of multilingual translation which emerged was quite separate from situational needs. Such a large number of languages could no longer be used for drafting purposes, and common sense suggested that one language should be used for drafting, and as a source language for the other language versions. This practice has proved successful as regards circumstantial needs and economic priorities, but it has developed without the support of any comparative evaluation or theoretical justification. The largest translation agency in the world can seemingly afford to ignore new translation trends and cultural orientations for historical reasons: the equal value of all language versions is based on political consensus but it is not clarified by a language policy explaining why the equivalence relation between the different versions is better served by a system of multilingual translation rather than multilingual drafting.

Political consensus over the illusion of language equality will be accepted if the language versions produced by multilingual translation are seen as being really equivalent. But when neither the writers nor the readers feel that this is the case, the issue of multilingualism is likely to be re-opened within the translation profession, and in political quarters, especially when the prospect of future enlargements may be leading the EU to make decisions regarding costs over quality, and when new initiatives such as *Citizens First* stipulate that communication with the general public must be improved, and greater attention be paid to text transparency with a wider use of ordinary, non-technical, language.

The perception of the inter-relatedness of the challenges of multilingual translation and the complex field of multilingualism has increased among European translators over the last decade. This book (gathering as it does the views of specialists in multilingual policies and in translation practices) was consequently designed to take stock of the work underway and of the on-going debate in the profession. Important elements are related to the change in status and content of the *Terminologie & Traduction*, the periodical compiled by translators working for the Commission and the Parliament. One could say that, whilst in the past this journal tended to represent the predominant view that multilingual translation is about finding terminological equivalences, in recent years it has began to stress the view that most problems of translation cannot be resolved, or even understood, without reference to the many contrasts between the principle and the practice of the EU policy of multilingualism. There are of course other positive signs that the cultural versus the technical perception of translation will increase in the future, as will the critical versus a passive attitude towards multilingualism. There are possibly historical and geographical reasons in Europe today. Some observers say that the planned enlargements will affect the awareness of the profession as the role and status of new, and possibly of the old, languages are restructured. Others think that wider mobility within the Union will change future generations of translators, who will have more linguistic awareness and be more sensitive to intercultural issues because of their own mixed backgrounds.

European developments will also have an impact on the perceptions of future MEPs, on the political alliances between Member States and across national divisions. It is impossible, however, to predict how far future enlargements and increased mobility will modify the current view that translation is little more than a technical operation, involving the identification of terminological equivalences rather than a skill requiring intercultural mediation between different national traditions. While some years ago discussions might have envisaged a united front against the hegemony of English, the future scenario remains unpredictable because the linguistic alliances are not evident, as they are rarely completely separate from political considerations. Certainly, the linguistic ambitions of some countries, who wish to defend the international role of their national language, do not necessarily coincide with the linguistic needs of smaller countries, who might find another language more accessible, although they themselves wish to safeguard the status of their national language at least at European level. This is the case for all Nordic countries, whose entry into the Union has greatly increased the status of English and its function in the translation system as the predominant language at the expense of French. Accordingly, France resents this loss of status; but the Nordic countries have given a better example by leading the campaign not in favour of one language, at the expense of another, but for more efficient translation and better communication (see, for example, Koskinen, 2000).

Most Member States from southern Europe could profitably join the Nordic campaign for a EU that 'speaks with a clearer voice in all national languages' but some are caught between their traditional membership to the Romance area, which in the past meant support of the French cause, and their new vested interest in the leadership of English. This attitude has increased the isolation of French but paradoxically has also spread international belief in the French oversimplification that all communication problems within 'Europe that speaks with one voice in many languages' are related to the predominance of English. Generally speaking, the stronger the nationalistic attitudes of politicians and the puristic attitudes of linguists of a given country become, the more difficult it is to present the problem of translation in Europe from a multilingual and multicultural perspective.

The message of this book is that of the conclusions of the first Seminar on Multilingualism organised by the Translation Service of the European Parliament at the end of 1998. Translators are increasingly aware of the institutional constraints on their professionalism, but they need the support of the European Parliament, and of the politicians and linguists, in their national communities, in order to encourage the largest translation agency in the world to rethink the role of translators, and to help it to spread a new translation culture in support of multilingualism in Europe.

## Reference
Koskinen, K. (2000) Translating in the EU Commission. *The Translator* 6 (1), 49–65.

# *The European Community's Language Charter*

---

**The Community's Language Charter**

Council Regulation No. 1 determining the languages to be used
by the European Economic Community (as amended)

THE COUNCIL OF THE EUROPEAN ECONOMIC COMMUNITY

Having regard to Article 217 of the Treaty which provides that the rules
governing the languages of the institutions of the Community shall,
without prejudice to the provisions contained in the rules of proceedings
of the Court of Justice, be determined by the Council, acting unani-
mously:

Whereas each of the nine languages in which the Treaty is drafted is
recognised as an official language in one or more of the Member State of
the Community.

HAS ADOPTED THIS REGULATION:

*Article 1*

The official languages and the working languages of the institutions of
the Community shall be Danish, Dutch, English, French, German, Greek,
Italian, Portuguese and Spanish.

*Article 2*

Documents which a Member State or a person subject to the jurisdiction
of a Member State sends to institutions of the Community may be drafted
in any one of the official languages selected by the sender. The reply shall
be drafted in the same language.

---

*Article 3*

Documents which an institution of the Community sends to a Member State or to a person subject to the jurisdiction of a Member State shall be drafted in the language of such State.

*Article 4*

Regulations and other documents of general application shall be drafted in the nine official languages.

*Article 5*

The *Official Journal of the European Communities* shall be published in the nine official languages.

*Article 6*

The institutions of the Community may stipulate in their rules of procedure which of the languages are to be used in specific cases.

*Article 7*

The languages to be used in the proceedings of the Court of Justice shall be laid down in its rules of procedure.

*Article 8*

If a Member State has more than one official language, the language to be used shall, at the request of such State, be governed by the general rules of its law.

This Regulation shall be binding in its entirety and directly applicable in all Member States.

# Index of Names

Ong, W. 88, 98
Ortega y Gasset, J. 38, 44
Orwell, G. 69,

Parlow, E. 122
Peyró, F. 112-113
Pinson, E.N. 10, 20
Plassart, P. 30
Plato 93
Plon, M. 22-24, 37
Pries, O. 112, 113
Prodi, R. 5, 55, 66

Quatrepoint, J.M. 30

Ramonet, I. 21-23
Rollason, C. xi, xv, 21, 117
Roudinesco, E. 22-24, 37
Roth, P. 22
Rushdie, S. 33, 37

Scarpetta, G. 22-24, 37
Seymour, E. xv, 43, 111-113
Smith, M.V. 124, 127
Snell-Hornby, M. 41, 44
Socrates 93

Sørensen, B. 112-113
Splinder, H. 112
Steiner, G. 45-46, 48-49, 66
Swallow, H. xv, 104

Tilotta, A. 111
Tomasi, L. xiii, xv, 88
Tosi, A. ix, xii, xv, 20, 66, 100, 102, 117, 120, 122, 126, 128
Trim, J. x, xi, xii, xv, 8, 17, 20, 50, 110, 122, 123, 126
Tucker, A. xiii, xv, 73, 88
Tytler, A. 45, 46, 66

Valery, P. 46
Vitanza, F. 112
Volman, Y. 44
Voltaire 35

Wagner, E. xv
Warin, O. 24, 27, 31, 37
William of Bessyngton 15
Wilson, B. ix, xiv, 1, 54, 66, 105, 120, 121
Wohlgemuth, F. 113

Young, H. 37, 35